Effective Questioning Strategies in the Classroom

A Step-by-Step Approach to Engaged Thinking and Learning, K–8

Effective Questioning Strategies in the Classroom

A Step-by-Step Approach to Engaged Thinking and Learning, K–8

Esther Fusco

Foreword by Lawrence F. Lowery

TEACHERS COLLEGE PRESS

Teachers College, Columbia University
New York and London

Published by Teachers College Press, 1234 Amsterdam Avenue, New York, NY 10027

Library of Congress Cataloging-in-Publication Data

Fusco, Esther.
    Effective questioning strategies in the classroom : a step-by-step approach to engaged thinking and learning, K-8 / Esther Fusco ; foreword by Lawrence F. Lowery.
        p. cm.
    Includes bibliographical references and index.
    ISBN 978-0-8077-5329-3 (pbk. : alk. paper)
        1. Questioning. 2. Critical thinking—Study and teaching (Elementary)
    3. Critical thinking—Study and teaching (Middle school) I. Title.
    LB1027.44.F87 2012
    371.3'7—dc23   2011048285

ISBN 978-0-8077-5329-3 (paperback)

Printed on acid-free paper
Manufactured in the United States of America

19 18 17 16 15 14 13 12   8 7 6 5 4 3 2 1

This book is dedicated to my husband, Andrew, and my children, their spouses, and my grandchildren: Chris, Beth, Andrea, Jason, Emilia, Andrew, Christopher, Caroline, Jessica, Jacqueline, and Alexander. My professional career has been filled with many wonderful opportunities. I have loved every moment of it. I hope my children and grandchildren feel the same about their choices and professions. It is a great way to spend a life.

Contents

Foreword

I recently observed an expert teacher while she was engaged with a student during a mathematics lesson. What I heard and saw was this:

The teacher sat next to the student and asked, "How much would you have if you added 10 and 10?"

The student replied, "20."

The teacher then asked, "How much would you have by adding 9 and 9?"

The student answered, "19."

The teacher next asked the student to tell her how he got 19.

And the student said, "Well, I know that 9 is 1 less than 10, so if 10 and 10 are 20, then 9 and 9 must be 19."

The teacher than asked, "If 9 and 9 are 19, how much would 10 and 9 be?"

The student thought for a moment, and then said with a smile, "They can't be the same. I see now. I forgot to take 1 more away for the second 9!"

This transaction lasted about 20 seconds, but in that short time the teacher orchestrated a questioning strategy that enabled the student to learn a mathematical idea through his own reasoning. The teacher did not "correct" the boy's "incorrect" answer. To her, the answer was not as important as the student's thinking; thus she asked a question that assessed his thinking. When he told her how he derived his answer, she then had data about his thinking, and because she knew her subject well, she gave him an appropriate comparison problem to ponder. The teacher never made a judgment of the boy's unexpected answer and did not try to show him what was faulty with his thinking. She decided it was more powerful to enable the student to derive the answer for himself along with an understanding of what he had neglected to do. She did this through the effective use of thoughtful questions.

I am willing to bet that the student learned more than a "correct" answer to a math problem, and that he will not make the same type of reasoning "error" again.

The book you are reading is about questions and the strategic use of them. My long-time friend and colleague, Esther Fusco, has spent a major part of her career in both the practical world of teaching and learning and the academic world of research about thinking and learning. The blend of these career experiences gave her the conviction that good thinking and learning can be enhanced through thoughtful questions as a normal and comfortable element of educational practice.

In this book she shows what effect different types of questions have on aspects of cognitive and affective thinking. Building on her own practical experiences and research studies on classroom questions, Esther outlines a range of teacher-initiated and student-initiated questions, from narrow, focused questions to broad, open-ended questions that excite the learner's curiosity and imagination and lead to inquiries, diverse ideas, knowledge, and solutions to problems.

You will enjoy this book. Esther writes in a friendly, conversational style. And since the ability to ask effective questions is a skill, she has included ways for you to try out and practice the kinds of questions that are introduced.

If you are serious about improving your knowledge about questions and your skill in using them, this is the book for you. Putting some time and effort into the suggested practice will be personally rewarding, and your students will benefit greatly from your effective use of questions.

—Lawrence F. Lowery, Professor Emeritus
Graduate School of Education, University of California at Berkeley

Acknowledgments

As I began to write this acknowledgment, I realized that the seed for this book was planted when I went to Brandeis University and took a course with Herman Epstein from Brandeis University and Patricia Arlin from the University of British Columbia. At the time, I had a MS degree, but Epstein and Arlin challenged my thinking, and I left Brandeis looking at my classroom teaching from a totally different developmental perspective. I knew I needed to learn more and to share what I had discovered with my colleagues.

Armed with this perspective, I brought the idea back to my principal, Dennis Littky of the Met Schools, who helped me establish a district-wide professional development course at Shoreham Wading River Central School District (NY) on cognition and teaching from a developmental perspective. Teaching others about this perspective forced me to totally renew my own teaching and questioning strategies that support the thinking and learning of my students. At the same time, I decided to begin a doctoral program at Hofstra University, and my advisor Harvey Alpert encouraged me to do research on questioning. As the success of the program at Shoreham Wading River grew, I worked with teams of professionals to help teachers in other school districts across the country grow in this perspective.

Two members of the teams who helped design the courses were Carole Noren, a director of special education, and Gwen Fountain, a former president of Butler University. They encouraged me to put the ideas that we were developing into writing. Carole has read and re-read the chapters of this book, as has my wonderful husband, Andrew Fusco. Andrew has always been my chief supporter. Finally, I had the good fortune to work with Douglas Gordon, who provided a critical but nurturing view of the book. I feel very fortunate to have all these wonderful people in my life. What I have learned from the process is that ideas take time and effort to develop and that we should never stop examining and sharing our beliefs.

Introduction

Good questions outrank easy answers.

—Paul A. Samuelson

Watch the dynamics of a vibrant classroom. What you will observe is a teacher skillfully asking effective questions. Teachers of all levels successfully use questions to transform their teaching. They use questions to encourage critical thinking skills, to effectively assess the nature of the learning, and to build the confidence of their students. When used properly in classrooms, questions build memory, focus attention, create emotions, hook the learning, and build imagination.

The primary goal of this book is to provide K–8 teachers with a step-by-step guide for implementing a procedure known as the Questioning Cycle. This is a seven-step process in which the teacher plans questions, asks questions, allows for wait time, listens to students' responses, assesses students' responses, follows up on those responses with another question, and re-plans based on students' subsequent responses.

Good questioning strategies are considered part of best practice. Effective questions and the language interactions they produce build students' thinking by encouraging students to reflect on their ideas and to compare their perceptions with those of others. Yet not all questions posed by a teacher are useful. For questions to be an effective tool, they need to stimulate active learning and connect to the students' background knowledge. Effective questioning:

- encourages students' discovery of new interests and increases their awareness of the potential of ideas and concepts;
- promotes deeper thinking about ideas, concepts, and beliefs; and
- creates a safe climate for diverse perspectives in classroom discussions.

My experiences as a teacher, administrator, and professional developer tell me that while there are many benefits to using effective questioning in a classroom, there still remains a wide gap between theory and practice. Much of classroom questioning practice continues to be mere recitation. Teachers I have observed see questions as an instrument to be used only when a specific answer is sought. They ask questions only when they already know the precise answers. This type of questioning discourages the act of discovery that good questioning seeks to promote.

The heart of a question is a controversy, a debate, and the consideration of an inquiry or issue. In fact, questioning strategies in teaching hark back to the Greek philosopher Socrates, who was described by his student Plato in the *Socratic Dialogues*. The so-called Socratic Method is a dialogue that is designed to consider deep puzzles and even contradictions. For example, the notion that "courage is always good" can be contradicted by the question, "Should one follow a general even if he is a madman?"—a question meant to expose the dangers of misplaced courage. Sometimes, in an effective discussion the contradiction remains and a conclusion is not reached.

This essential questioning seldom occurs in classes today. One reason is that teachers, especially middle grade and high school teachers, feel pressured to cover extensive content for state tests. Although they may ask questions, they do so merely to check that students have retained the basic facts. In school after school, you can observe a teacher pass over a student who has answered "incorrectly" or even finish the student's response, not allowing the student to elaborate. In such cases, the teacher has missed the point of effective questioning. The opportunity for a thoughtful discussion has been lost. Consider what might happen if, instead of overlooking a student with the incorrect answer, the teacher asked, "Tell me why you think that. What is your evidence?" Quite possibly, the student's follow-up response would open up a totally different and important aspect of the topic that the teacher had not considered.

The Questioning Cycle is a strategy that breaks the rigid, traditional pattern of recitation and memorization. Instead, it provides an organizational framework that enables teachers to plan purposeful questions that get at the heart of a lesson, that encourage a diversity of ideas, and that

Teacher Reflection: Change

What has changed for me is my whole attitude in asking questions. I thought I could only ask kindergarten children straight fact questions—strictly recitation. Now, I know better and understand how the back-and-forth elaboration on a question stretches their thinking.

—Kindergarten teacher

build an interactive classroom culture that supports creative and critical thinking. It is a well-proven technique that I have repeatedly seen foster reflection and stronger questioning skills in both teachers and students as it transforms a monotonous classroom into a lively forum.

THE IMPORTANCE OF QUESTIONING STRATEGIES

Teachers who use questions effectively can testify to the fact that students become more curious and actively involved with learning when they feel free to demonstrate their thinking skills and when they can question, examine, and argue about different aspects of the topic at hand. Perhaps unsurprisingly, students can also learn to become better listeners through questioning. They learn how to be respectful toward ideas that might be different from their own because they have to patiently listen and evaluate the evidence at hand before responding. Their responses might be supportive or challenging, but the cognitive shift and modified perspectives they undergo are critical elements of what we call *learning*. Often, such discussions are fruitful and can even be exhilarating; they are the best way to encourage students to become reflective and responsible thinkers.

In the following discussion, notice how a 4th-grade teacher encourages students to think through an idea and build on the comments of their peers.

Questions in the Classroom: Different Perspectives

TEACHER: Why are books important to us?

SHEILA: Because they are fun.

TEACHER: Are all books fun?

SHEILA: When I pick them, they are.

MAURI: Sometimes, books are not fun but interesting.

TEACHER: What do you mean?

MAURI: They have ideas, like when we were doing our alphabet books for kindergarten. You read *Aster Aardvark's Alphabet Adventures*. That was interesting.

JAMES: Yeah, Steven Kellogg used each letter of the alphabet to take Aster through his adventures. We made our books like that, too.

SHELLY: To me, that book was fun and interesting. But you can have books that are interesting but not fun, like when we read *Messages in the Mailbox: How to Write a Letter*. It helped us with writing letters to our pen pals. I learned the parts of a letter. I needed that.

JAMES: Not me. I didn't like it. I already knew that information. So it
  wasn't important for me.
TEACHER: Let's see if we can create a list of reasons why books may be
  important.

The discussion started with a question rather than an assertion. The
teacher's follow-up response to the comment that "books are not fun but
interesting" allowed the student to respond again. This invited further
elaboration on the idea about the content of books. Because the students
were used to follow-up questions, they easily interacted with one another's comments. Other questions the teacher might have asked are, "What
qualities make a book important?" and "Can you describe the writing
styles you find interesting?" The teacher could have also broadened the
conversation and learned more about students' specific reading interests.
All of these are possible in a classroom that encourages questions as the
basis for thinking and learning.

Because the Questioning Cycle focuses on constructing and using
knowledge rather than passively accepting unexamined information, it
has far-reaching consequences. As we prepare our students for success in
the future, we are aware of the complexity and uncertainty they face in
the ever-changing, fast-paced world they will enter. Providing them with
a solid cognitive foundation that supports critical thinking and problem-
solving is our major responsibility as teachers. At its best, the Questioning
Cycle stimulates confident and creative problem-solving, and it generates
the necessary skills that students need to become informed citizens who
are able to develop and express their ideas and even tolerate or incorporate divergent opinions. This is a learning model that will help students
make decisions in the best interests of their individual lives, their community, and the wider world.

According to Andrew, a 5th-grader in a Virginia school that I visited,
"I make better choices since I have been in Mr. B's class. I look at things
carefully and don't judge as quickly."

Let's look at another example in a 2nd-grade classroom where the
teacher was working on developing the concept of friendship and the
skill of comparisons. The teacher began with an "I wonder" statement
that allowed the student to logically explain his conceptual appreciation
of diversity.

Questions in the Classroom: Building Understanding

TEACHER: We have discussed the book and poem on friendship. I am
  now curious. . . .I wonder if it is possible for people who are
  different to be friends.

JARED: Of course.

TEACHER: You say that so convincingly. Tell me why you think that.

JARED: Christopher and I are different. Look at our Venn diagrams. We have only one thing alike. We both have brown hair. But he still is my friend. And [he] is special, like the poem says.

TEACHER: What makes him special?

JARED: Christopher looks different and can do things that I can't do. It would be boring if we were the same. When we work together, he helps me. Sometimes I help him. That makes us both special.

TEACHER: Does that mean all your friends are different from you?

JARED: Some are like me in some ways, but mostly they are not.

TEACHER: Can you summarize then what makes you friends?

JARED: What I like about my friendship with Christopher is that we are different. We help each other by thinking of different ideas or games. I think I like Christopher because he isn't like me. Our differences make us special because we are not the same.

Notice from this example that teachers can ask questions either directly or in the form of a statement that accomplishes the same thing. The "I wonder" statement is essentially a question, and so is "Tell me why you think that." With these statements and with her direct questions later on in the discussion, the teacher drew out the student's ideas, encouraged him to think deeply about friendship, and helped develop his skill in drawing comparisons and contrasts.

THE IMPACT OF QUESTIONING ON TEST-TAKING

Some teachers may be reluctant to employ the Questioning Cycle because they believe it will take too much time. Under pressure to raise students' scores on standardized tests, they feel their precious class hours should focus strictly on the skills and knowledge required by the tests. This narrow "teaching to the test" perspective too often stunts students' intellectual growth without producing significant improvements in test scores.

Research suggests, in fact, that effective questioning not only enhances the classroom atmosphere but also produces superior test results. In 2000, the National Reading Panel verified that text comprehension, as measured by standardized comprehension tests, improves when students have experience with questions that explore knowledge at different levels. The panel also noted how important it is for students to think about what they have read and to ask their own questions about it (National Institute of Child Health and Human Development, 2000).

From classroom discussions, students learn that answers might not be obvious from the content and instead might need to be constructed. This insight is then applied to their own reading, and especially to test-taking. Students know that they may have to think about the information and then change, modify, or extend it in order to structure a response. The Questioning Cycle thus helps raise the performance level of students by expanding their cognitive skills so that test-taking becomes an opportunity to succeed rather than fail. For example, in a discussion with his teacher after he took a state test, 5th-grader Jason said:

> I had an easier time with the test because I am used to your asking us questions that are not in the book. You do that all the time, so the test was pretty easy because I knew that I had to put the information together in my mind to come up with the answers. The stories gave the ideas, but I had to think about what [the test-makers] meant when they asked the questions, because [the answers] were not exactly there.

THE PREMISES OF THIS BOOK

The underlying premises of this book are based upon the writings of Jean Piaget, John Dewey, and L. S. Vygotsky, all of whom have written extensively on the active learning process. My own philosophical premise is that students' cognitive development increases as they have the opportunity to use their thinking strategies in relevant learning situations. As students examine new information, they integrate and evaluate it in light of their own previous experiences. As they exchange this information in meaningful experiences, they construct a schema, or a mental filing system, that they can adjust or modify as the new information is considered. In this interactive learning model, both the information and the student are transformed. The model is founded on the notion that learning depends on what a student already knows, as well as how willing he or she is to engage in the learning process. The student's prior knowledge may vary, but in all cases the individual learner should be actively engaged in the process of constructing knowledge.

Hilda Taba, a well-known pioneer in the field of social studies, concluded that the most important factor in developing students' cognitive ability was the extensive use of questioning strategies (Taba, Levine, & Elzey, 1964). Surely, developing students' cognitive skills is a priority for all teachers. This book is designed to help teachers improve their questioning strategies so that they can help their students develop critical thinking

---

Teacher Reflection: Suggestion

Your suggestion to tape my lesson and listen to my questioning techniques was eye-opening. I realized that I ask few questions overall. Also, the types of questions asked were far more literal than I expected. I also did not spread them out [among] the range of students, both male and female, and [their] various abilities. I think this shows my need to focus my approach and set a goal to redesign my questioning strategies.

—8th-grade social studies teacher

---

skills, get the most out of their learning, and become responsive members of the classroom community.

THE STRUCTURE OF THIS BOOK

The chapters in this book include several components that are designed to actively involve the reader. These include:

- *Questions in the Classroom:* As you have already seen, these are transcribed examples of questioning in an actual classroom setting. Some of the examples come from the author's own interaction and taped lessons with students. Others come from taped lessons submitted to the author by students in her undergraduate and graduate education courses. Still other examples derive from the author's observations of teachers in the classroom with students. Each example is meant to shed more light on the aspect of the Questioning Cycle that is described in Chapter 1. It is useful to note the type of questions that are asked in these examples and how the students respond and build on one another's ideas. A sense of community is often revealed as the students reflect and share their ideas in meaningful discussions that include the teacher.
- *Teacher Reflection:* These include an excerpt from a student teacher's or practicing teacher's reflective writing. Each of these passages reflects the teacher's insight into his or her learning experiences.
- *Action Items:* These are suggested activities designed to provide teachers with tasks that may facilitate their own teaching.

Because reflection is a part of the self-improvement process, you should find it helpful to respond to the items at the ends of the chapters, especially if you do so in collaboration with a colleague or study group.

Action Items

1. Discuss with a colleague how each of you uses questions in your lessons. Inquire about any special training the other teacher had with this strategy. What are the similarities and differences in your approaches?
2. Consider and respond to the following statements and whether they are true of your current practice or may be areas in which you need to adjust your practice or build your skills. This will give you a foundation for reading this book and it will allow you to assess your progress along the way.

    a. My questions relate to the focus questions in my lessons.
    b. I am flexible with the questions I plan. I do not have to use all the questions I plan, nor do I use them in the exact way I planned.
    c. My questions reflect my awareness of my students' background knowledge.
    d. I provide wait time after each question.
    e. I follow up my questions with related questions.
    f. I repeat questions to various students to get diverse opinions.
    g. I encourage students to ask questions of me and others.
    h. I encourage student-to-student interactions during our discussions.
    i. When my questions and student questions are complete, I have evidence of what knowledge the students have gained and a better sense of where to go next with my lesson.
    j. My students eagerly participate in our classroom discussions.

CHAPTER ONE

The Questioning Cycle

The fool wonders, the wise man asks.

—Chinese proverb

Let's begin with a snapshot of suburban students in a literature group discussing the topic of discrimination. This example demonstrates how 6th-grade students build knowledge and marshal their evidence as they engage in a discussion about the classic book *Sounder* by William Armstrong (1969).

Questions in the Classroom: Developing Students' Thinking

TEACHER: How does the boy's father get the ham?

HADI: He steals it.

TEACHER: Can you tell us more about that?

HADI: The sheriff and his deputy come to the house and the ham was cooking.

TEACHER: Describe what happens.

HADI: They threw the ham on the floor and all the children were backed up against the fireplace and they put handcuffs on them.

TEACHER: As you read this part, what was your reaction?

CLAIRE: I didn't understand how a sheriff could handcuff the children. They were not involved in the stealing.

TEACHER: What evidence did they have that there was stealing?

ORLANDO: Well, they said the father got his pants ripped and they found threads on plants or something . . . and what is that house called where they keep all the meat? They found it had been robbed.

CLAIRE: But that was the father, not the kids.

ORLANDO: Yeah, but that didn't matter to those types of people. They didn't care about the kids.

TEACHER: What do you mean, "those types of people"?

ORLANDO: The ones who are prejudiced.

TEACHER: Let's read over this section and see if we can find evidence that the police are prejudiced or explain why the children are handcuffed. Remember, the information doesn't have to be right there. It can be implied from what you find in the passages.

In this example, the teacher uses the discussion of *Sounder* to probe students and encourage them to look for evidence for their ideas. As the dialogue demonstrates, a question is not an instrument to be used only when a specific answer is sought. In this discussion, the teacher uses questions as a tool to develop thinking, which—along with specific knowledge acquisition—is part of what we call cognitive development.

In her questions about the incident in *Sounder*, the teacher wanted students to determine why the sheriff would handcuff the children and to examine the author's purpose in including the scene. Good questioning strategies like this enable teachers to assess students' knowledge and their ability to link their thoughts with broader concepts. Students become more excited and actively involved when their curiosity is piqued, and they feel free to use their thinking skills to question, examine, and argue about different aspects of the concepts at hand. There is no single, simple answer to why the sheriff would handcuff the children, but listing all the possible reasons was fascinating for the students and informative for the teacher.

ACTIVE PROCESSING

In John Dewey's early book *How We Think* (1991), he proposed the idea that learning should be an active, reflective process, one that engages students' thinking about real issues and ideas. Since his writing, many scholars have continued to advocate for a paradigm of active learning, reflection, and questioning that shifts from a mundane, factual approach to one that emphasizes rigorous thinking and processing of information. One purpose of the Questioning Cycle is to create a classroom environment that invites the students to consider ideas and ask meaningful questions about them.

In *Brain Matter: Translating Research into Classroom Practice*, Patricia Wolfe (2001) advocates "hands-on" experiences that have real purpose. She adds that active learning is valuable as long as it is also "minds-on" for students (p. 188). The same might be said about questions: We want the questions to engage our students to think and to participate in a process that *moves beyond the factual to more demanding cognitive processing*. For some teachers, questions and the responses they yield can become the most critical aspect of their teaching. These exchanges are used to assess their students and thus guide subsequent instruction.

As you read the next classroom interaction, think about the 3rd-grader's reaction. How does this compare with responses you have heard from students?

Questions in the Classroom: Changing Perspectives

TEACHER: Why do I ask questions?
CHRISTOPHER: So you can check up on us.
TEACHER: What do you mean, check up on you?
CHRISTOPHER: To see if we are learning anything.
TEACHER: Are you saying that, when I ask you a question, it is like my giving you a test or quiz?
CHRISTOPHER: Yup.
TEACHER: What if I said I ask questions to learn from you? I want to know how you are thinking about what we are learning.
CHRISTOPHER: I would have to think about that.
TEACHER: Why?
CHRISTOPHER: Because I never thought about it that way. I thought you were checking up on whether we were listening to you. I didn't think you were interested in my thinking.

In my discussion with the teacher after this interaction, she indicated that she had to reevaluate her teaching because of Christopher's comment. She recognized that she was missing aspects of the questioning process. In fact, she acknowledged that Christopher was probably right in his thinking and that she therefore needed to do a better job with questioning.

WHAT IS THE QUESTIONING CYCLE?

The Questioning Cycle is a systematic method for using questions to collect information about students' knowledge, encourage students to consider diverse ideas, and build a community of thinkers. The basic steps in the Questioning Cycle are:

- Establishing lesson goals and guiding questions
- Planning the question
- Asking the question
- Allowing wait time
- Listening to the student's response

- Assessing the student's response
- Following up the student's response with another question
- Re-planning based on students' responses

This process is illustrated in Figure 1.1.

During the Questioning Cycle, the teacher uses his or her planned questions to stimulate the conversation about the information being taught, and the discussion allows students to reveal their real understanding of the concepts being explored. When teachers begin to consistently ask challenging questions to students, there is a change in students' understanding of the concepts (Fusco, 1983). Students begin to search inwardly for more information, piggyback on the ideas of their classmates' responses, and establish more of a community atmosphere. Later chapters in this book examine each of the steps in the cycle. The rest of this chapter considers the attributes that make questions effective and the overall process of using the strategy in your classroom.

Figure 1.1. Steps in the Questioning Cycle

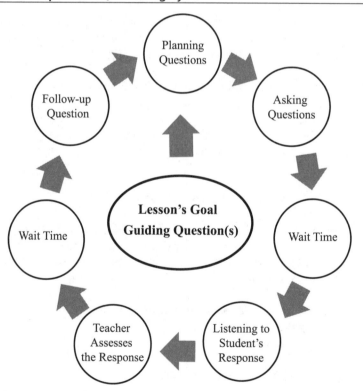

THE ATTRIBUTES OF QUESTIONS

In and of themselves, questions do not necessarily affect learning, particularly if they focus on isolated points that might (or might not) build the memorization skills of students. Such questions can be disconnected, often literal in nature, and may not relate to the learner's background. If we want to create a classroom that is stimulating, one that provides enrichment for the brain, then we need to ask many questions that do not just elicit "yes" or "no" answers. We must ask questions that students need to contemplate and draw conclusions from. Such a paradigm shifts the teaching away from rote memorization toward the acquisition of more meaningful concepts and skills (Erlauer, 2003).

It is important to remember that questions should build on current knowledge and occur in a relevant context. Teachers need to appreciate and share with their students the idea that questions have particular *contexts*, *purposes*, and *levels*. After I completed a presentation at a national conference on the Questioning Cycle, a 6th-grade teacher stopped by to speak with me. Distressed, she began with the fact that she had been teaching for 10 years and had a master's degree. She was frustrated because, in all that time, no one had ever spoken with her about the attributes of questions. The following sections explore the question attributes that we discussed at that conference.

The Context of Questions

To grasp the full context of a question, think about matters like these:

- What relationship does the question have to the subject?
- How does the question relate to the main concepts that are being developed?
- What background knowledge do the students have to help them understand the question?
- How is the question connected to other questions?

In our previous example of the discussion of *Sounder*, the setting is a 6th-grade social studies and language arts unit. The context of the reading is an examination of the South during the 19th century, and the class is considering what happened to poor minorities during this time period. The overall themes are poverty, discrimination, and injustice in our society. The teacher planned questions that built on the students' knowledge and encouraged an exploration of the way the story relates to the larger themes. Planning is a vital part of effective instructional practice.

The Purpose of Questions

Teachers employ questioning in a variety of ways and for different reasons. These may include merely ensuring that students have understood the basic points of a lesson. Or, according to William Wilen (1991), the purposes for asking questions might be to stimulate student participation; to initiate discussion of a topic, issue, or problem based on previous learning; and to evaluate students' preparation for a later learning task.

For me, questions are critical strategies to differentiate instruction and promote diversified interactions among students. In my own teaching, I have found that questions have a profoundly positive impact on students' cognitive and emotional development. Encouraged by a teacher's questions, students come to trust that the teacher will listen and respond to their answers in a nurturing way. Experienced teachers know that students recognize when someone is actually listening and responding to their thinking, and students also realize that they themselves are developing a clearer understanding of a concept and growing in knowledge. When this occurs, they become more actively engaged. They feel excited and empowered, and they begin to apply this understanding and self-confidence to a broader range of topics. In the following discussion, a 3rd-grade boy describes his reactions to the questioning process.

Questions in the Classroom: Reflective Questions

NICOLE: I like 3rd grade better than 2nd grade.
TEACHER: Why is that?
NICOLE: We get to talk more and I like to talk.
TEACHER: Are you saying I let you talk all the time?
NICOLE: No, but you ask us a lot of stuff and we get to talk about it. I talk a lot, but so does everyone.
TEACHER: When I ask you about stuff and you listen to your classmates talk, what happens?
NICOLE: Sometimes I learn and my ideas change, but sometimes I disagree, and then there is a problem.
TEACHER: Why is that?
NICOLE: Because it is hard not to say to someone, you are wrong. I don't like to be wrong, and sometimes it's not wrong, it's just a different way to look at the question. You know what I mean?

This interaction with the student reinforced the teacher's effort to use questions on a regular basis. He realized that his students had become

---

Teacher Reflection: Observing Children

I have definitely noticed a change in how the children respond to questions. There are some children who raise their hands right away because that is what they think they have to do. When I see that children are raising their hands right away and I want them to think more, I let them know that it is all right to take their time and think. This also allows a few more seconds for everyone to think. Now, I am seeing more of my children answering questions, even the shy children. They know that they have the time they need to think about their responses. They know that most of the questions require them to put the information together in some way. They know it, yet they still engage in the discussion trying out their ideas and using their background knowledge. It is quite a change, especially for my students who still for the most part have difficulty with abstract thinking. I am using the Questioning Cycle to help me build their reasoning skills.

—6th-grade teacher

---

comfortable when he asked them to think and respond to the questions he posed. He recognized that questioning was an opportunity to build his students' knowledge.

Along these lines, we can say that the purpose of the questions in the *Sounder* example was to help the students develop an understanding of racism in the 19th-century South. Each specific question encouraged the students to consider the details of the plot, explore their reactions, and examine the text more deeply to discover its significance.

The Types of Questions

Along with a question's purpose and context, we should consider its type. There are three different types of questions, literal, inferential, and metacognitive, as illustrated in Figure 1.2.

Literal questions ask for specific answers. They are often designed to elicit recalled information, to request only the facts, and to bring forth information that is explicitly stated or "right there" in the text or lesson (Raphael, 1982). Questions of this type are often called "closed questions" because they have only one right answer. Examples of literal questions are:

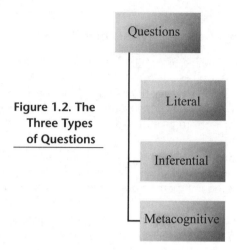

**Figure 1.2. The
Three Types
of Questions**

- How many minutes are there in an hour?
- What season comes after fall?
- Who wrote *Tuck Everlasting*?
- Who was president of the United States in 2007?

By contrast, when teachers use *inferential questions*, they anticipate responses that are not directly stated in the text. They hope to encourage their students to go beyond the text and to manipulate the information in some way in order to construct an appropriate response. They want their students to think about what is directly stated, but they also want them to consider related, but not necessarily obvious, information and ideas. Such questions are often called "open-ended questions" because there is no single correct response and students are free to develop their own lines of reasoning. Examples of inferential questions are:

- How would you evaluate the accomplishments of our president?
- What would happen to plants in our area if we didn't have summer?
- What does *Tuck Everlasting* tell us about keeping a secret?

To clarify the distinction between literal and inferential questions, here are some paired examples:

- Who is in your family? (literal)
- What is a family? (inferential)
- Can you describe this apple? (literal)
- What are the benefits of eating an apple? (inferential)

- What is the name of your favorite fairy tale? (literal)
- What makes a story a fairy tale? (inferential)
- What is a hurricane? (literal)
- What is the impact of a hurricane? (inferential)

Using Literal and Inferential Questions

It is important to clarify when to use inferential questions (which usually demand more critical thinking) and when to use literal questions (which require memorization and recitation). Each type of question has value and should be used appropriately. There are certainly times when a teacher will want to use a literal question. For example, a literal question can help establish the factual foundation on which students can base their inferences. In that way, literal questions can serve as a warm-up to inferential questions. Returning to the *Sounder* discussion, notice how the teacher uses literal questions to build to inferential questions:

- How does the boy's father get the ham? (literal)
- As you read this part, what was your reaction? (inferential)
- What evidence did they have that there was stealing? (literal)
- Let's read over this section and see if we can find evidence that the police are prejudiced or explain why the children are handcuffed. (inferential)

Since the goal of the Questioning Cycle is to assist teachers who want to go beyond the memorization of factual information, inferential questions play a large role in the process of helping students read and understand complex texts. In the *Sounder* example, the 6th-grade teacher decided to use the Questioning Cycle strategy to help students develop their ability to think abstractly—that is, to develop their *inferential knowledge and reasoning*. In order to do this, the teacher needed to move away from literal questions to inferential questions that encouraged the students to elaborate, clarify, and even summarize their thinking. The teacher used inferential questions to investigate more complex issues and seek multiple perspectives, to encourage students to present evidence for their answers, and to build a tone of acceptance of different ideas. This decision shifts the thinking of the students and the teacher. Using inferential questions is central to the Questioning Cycle and key to successfully employing the National Core Standards. As teachers begin to implement the Core Standards, there is the realization that giving evidence for responses and understanding text complexity is vital in the comprehension process. Systematically using inferential questions is key to supporting student development in this domain.

Using Metacognitive Questions

Along with literal and inferential questions, I believe teachers must also plan to use metacognitive questions, which encourage students to reflect on their own thinking and learning. By becoming more aware of their own thinking needs and processes, students build their cognitive skills. In the following example, the teacher guides a student into a metacognitive reflection on his own learning.

Questions in the Classroom: Reading Comprehension

ALEX: You said that we should always read the title first. But
    sometimes the title is confusing.
TEACHER: What do you mean, "confusing"?
ALEX: Well, it doesn't tell you what the book is really going to be
    about. It's not like a summary.
TEACHER: Would you like it to be a summary?
ALEX: No, 'cause that would be too long and silly for a title.
TEACHER: So, what exactly would you like?
ALEX: I would like more information so I can make better choices.
TEACHER: What else can we do after we read the title to help us
    understand what the book will be about?
ALEX: I don't know. That's why I ask the questions.
TEACHER: Can anyone give Alex any suggestions on what to do to
    know about a book beyond reading the title? Who can share
    their thinking on this?

In the conversation about book titles, Alex has to think about other ways he can gather information. To help him, the teacher uses questions to get Alex to become more reflective about his needs and to encourage Alex to invite his peers to help. Simply by asking Alex what else he could do, the teacher helps the youngster begin to develop an awareness that he needs to expand his strategies for approaching a new book.

Notice that the interaction ends in an open-ended way because Alex needs to think more about what is being discussed. In a questioning classroom, this is an important level to reach. All questions don't have to be answered immediately or by one student. Students can build their thinking over time and through the follow-up responses of their peers.

One outcome of the Questioning Cycle is that students begin to realize that they are responsible for their learning. They have to push their thinking. This shifts the dynamic of the classroom. Students become more tolerant when they listen to their peers struggle with ideas because they know they, too, have had the same experience. They also become more helpful and more eager to share their knowledge because they know that the follow-up part of the cycle encourages student-to-student interactions.

Finally, let's look at how a 4th-grade teacher uses these three types of questions as she plans a lesson with the Questioning Cycle. The teacher's goal is to have students compare and contrast the attributes of the planets and to eventually consider the idea of the potential for inhabiting another planet. If the students believe life is not possible on other planets, she hopes they will think about what we need to do with our own planet. She plans these questions for the lesson.

- Name the planets. (literal)
- Explain our definition of a planet. (literal)
- How are the planets alike and different? (inferential)
- Why is it important to know about the different planets? (inferential)
- What important qualities does the Earth have to support life? (literal)
- What evidence do we have about life on other planets? Do you believe this is possible? Why do you think this? (inferential)
- What conclusions can you come to about life on other planets? What is your evidence? (inferential)
- How should these ideas impact our way of life on our planet? (inferential)
- How do these ideas influence your thinking? (metacognitive)

Notice how she uses all three different types of questions. She also recognizes that these are the baseline questions and that the students' follow-up responses will ultimately determine the direction of the discussion. Clearly, this class has already engaged in lessons on the planets. When designing her inferential questions, the teacher has decided to give the students something to think about, an interesting topic, so she leads them toward a consideration of whether life is possible on other planets. She has taken into consideration the students' cognitive levels, the context, and the students' interest level based on their prior learning. Although demanding and time-consuming, her preparation of open-ended, inferential, and metacognitive questions is worth the effort because the students will grapple with significant ideas.

Charlotte Danielson (2007) states that it is difficult to overstate the importance of planning. In fact, one could go further and argue that a teacher's role is not so much to teach as it is to arrange for learning. That is, a teacher's essential responsibility is to ensure that students learn through designing (or selecting or adapting) learning activities that encourage students to explore important content. Thus, planning is a matter of design.

This type of designing is at the heart of effective questioning, and as teachers use it they begin to recognize how it makes the exchanges with students more creative.

USING THE QUESTIONING CYCLE IN YOUR CLASSROOM

Using the Questioning Cycle as a pedagogical strategy encourages teachers to shift more of their instruction toward ways in which students can actively process their experiences. As students begin to respond more often to questions that require them to create, invent, and design answers, teachers start to notice that students transfer these skills into all areas of instruction.

Figure 1.3, based on the work of Alvermann, Dillon, and O'Brien (1987), presents comparisons that you may find useful in making the transition from a "recitation" style of teaching that uses a small number of fact-oriented, literal questions to the Questioning Cycle, which challenges students with plenty of inferential and metacognitive questions.

Questions that are meant to inspire thoughtful reflection are especially important for student learning. In teaching, fostering reflection is essential for building a broad instructional framework. Once teachers begin to use the Questioning Cycle, they begin to notice that students are more reflective in their responses. In the beginning, though, it is helpful to inform the students that they are engaged in the Questioning Cycle. Tell

Figure 1.3. The Questioning Cycle Compared with the Recitation Model

Recitation	The Questioning Cycle
Students must respond with an answer the teacher has determined to be correct.	Students must present multiple points of view and then be ready to change their minds after hearing contrary convincing evidence.
Discussion is a one-to-one interaction between the teacher and a single student.	Students must interact with one another as well as with the teacher.
Most responses are two- to three-word phrases limited by previous learning.	Most verbal interactions must be longer than the typical two- or three-word phrases. All students are encouraged to elaborate on their individual responses.

Source: Adapted from Alvermann, Dillon, & O'Brien, 1987, p. 3.

them what it is and what is expected of them. Initially, they will need to be reminded that they are engaged in a conversation that will demand multiple responses and answers. From my own teaching, I have learned that students need this reminder several times over a couple of weeks. Because they are used to right and wrong answers, they tend to shy away when asked a follow-up question. The value of this reminder is that students begin to trust that the teacher will respond to their answers with a follow-up question, that there is going to be a dialogue, and that such a dialogue may even deepen their connection to the ideas of other students.

What I have consistently observed is that teachers who ask students to reflect and who help their students develop metacognitive skills also reflect themselves on what has just occurred and how it relates to their immediate teaching goals. This practice has been well described in Donald A. Schön's (1995) book *The Reflective Practitioner: How Professionals Think in Action*. Schön states that

> both ordinary people and professional practitioners often think about what they are doing, sometimes even while doing it. Stimulated by surprise, they turn thought back on action and on knowing, which is implicit in action. They may ask themselves: What procedures am I enacting when I perform this skill? How am I framing the problem that I am trying to solve? Usually reflection on knowing-in-action goes together with reflection on the stuff at hand. (p. 50)

Schön goes on to say that as we reflect, we try to understand what has "been implicit in our actions, that which is surface and that which needs to be criticized, restructured, and embodied in further action" (1995, p. 50).

Let's look at another discussion in a 5th-grade classroom where the students are involved with a unit on weather conditions in different environments.

Questions in the Classroom: Asking Questions

TEACHER: All your [raised] hands tell me you seem to have a lot of questions about this discussion about the effects on weather in different areas. Jessie, you had your hand up first. What is your question?

JESSIE: How does this apply when you get higher in the mountains?

TEACHER: What information have you learned so far that you can use to answer your own question?

JESSIE: I am guessing now, but the farther away you go from sea level, the colder it gets?

TEACHER: You're thinking that elevation plays a part in the mountains having cooler temperatures. What else?

PACO: Well, there is less air, because if you are flying and there is a problem in the airplane, you have to put on an oxygen mask. Probably the lack of oxygen at higher elevations makes it cooler.

TEACHER: That is a very interesting connection.

JESSIE: In the article we read, it said that the wind affected the climate, even in the desert. Is it windy in the mountains?

PACO: It can be windy in the desert and here in Florida where we live, yet we don't have snow.

YU: But when it is windy here, it usually cools us down so maybe it is windy in the mountains.

JESSIE: I have more questions. How can we tell if these are the right reasons? And what about the mountains near the equator? Are they cold, too?

TEACHER: What do we usually do when we have questions and information that we are not sure is correct?

YU: We have to do research, and I want to work with Jessie on this because I am curious now if we came up with all the right reasons and it is cooler in the mountains, and what about the deserts?

As this example shows, using questions to get students involved in a relevant discussion fosters a genuine desire to know more about the subject. This desire is often translated into greater effort on the part of the learner. This happens readily in a classroom where students are used to inferential and metacognitive questions and where they expect follow-up questions that are directly related to their responses. Students readily embrace the Questioning Cycle because they understand that the teacher is listening to their responses and thinking about what they are saying. This is empowering to students.

In Chapter 2, we will see how teachers begin the Questioning Cycle by planning the questions.

Action Items

1. In reviewing the Questioning Cycle, create a list of concerns that you think might impede the effectiveness or the flow of discussion in your classroom. Think about why you have these concerns.

2. What can you do to enhance the Questioning Cycle? How can you get the necessary support to assist you with the changes you would like to make?

3. As you read the following questions, jot down your answers so that you can revisit your thinking at a later time.

    a. Why do you use questioning strategies in your classroom?

    b. How do you develop questioning strategies?

    c. How do your questions promote thinking and build knowledge?

    d. How do your questions assess students' understanding of a concept?

    e. Do your questions promote a variety of student interactions in the classroom?

    f. What is your planning process?

    g. What do you observe in your classroom when you use questioning as a strategy?

    h. How do you evaluate the success of your questioning skills in a lesson?

CHAPTER TWO

Planning
Effective Questions

You can tell whether a man is clever by his answers. You can tell whether a man is wise by his questions.

—Naguib Mahfouz, Nobel Prize winner

In my conferencing with teachers, most recount that during some part of their educational program, they heard something about the different types of questions, but there were few if any demonstrations of how to use this information. What most teachers recall dates back to their student teaching and their observations of recitation as a response to questions. These were not situations that generated thought-provoking, lively discussions. By way of contrast, consider the following Questions in the Classroom, and notice how the student begins to apply his understanding to different situations in the schooling experience.

Questions in the Classroom: Making Connections

TEACHER: Thank you for taking your time to think about your answers. I would like you to do some more thinking. Can you add anything to your answer? How does this connect what we have discussed so far to something else we've learned?
ANDREW: Well, I was thinking that all Patricia Polacco's books so far are about people helping people.
TEACHER: Would you explain more about what you mean?
ANDREW: The characters are not in the same family, but they help one another. Like Larnel getting the cat for Mrs. Katz or the children getting the hat for Miss Eula. They helped even though they weren't family.
TEACHER: How does that idea connect to something for you?
ANDREW: Well, you tell us that we have to help each other. The story characters didn't need their teacher to tell them. They just knew to do it.

TEACHER: Let's brainstorm all the possible reasons that these characters knew that they should be helpful.

In building connections to the concept of helpfulness, the teacher motivated the student to move well beyond the text at hand. Though the teacher responded smoothly to the flow of the discussion, the questioning was not a spur-of-the-moment development; rather, the teacher did some careful planning beforehand to determine how best to use questions to guide the students' learning. This chapter begins the exploration of the elements involved in effective question planning.

THE ELEMENTS OF PLANNING

Planning effective questions is a complex process that is determined by a variety of instructional functions. Doug, a 5th-grade teacher, explained to me that he now designs his lessons differently and more systematically than he used to. Doug analyzes the concept and skills he will teach and then plans the questions he wants to ask accordingly. He creates three to five inferential questions to guide his lesson. These are connected to the background knowledge students have or are developing. Because time is a factor, he carefully selects questions that will go to the heart of the main ideas of the lesson. Doug notes that his students now achieve important learning outcomes more readily because his questions are well organized and are tied closely to his lesson objectives.

The key points in this approach are shown diagrammatically in Figure 2.1. Carefully constructed questions, like those Doug is now using, provide students with a chance to experience a spirited and supportive environment, one that provides an opportunity for them to apply their growing knowledge and problem-solving skills across disciplines. The goal of Doug's well-structured lesson is to ask a few thought-provoking, concept-building questions rather than many factual ones. As Sadker and Sadker (2003) say,

> Most teachers today ask too many questions. In fact, the typical teacher asks hundreds of questions a day. One way to improve teaching effectiveness becomes painfully obvious: ask fewer questions. While this may not sound particularly challenging, changing any habit, whether personal or professional, can be quite difficult. (p. 105)

Teachers need to ask fewer questions but devise ones that are designed to promote thinking and creativity of thought.

Figure 2.1. Steps in Planning Questions for a Lesson

Consider Goals, Objectives, and Guiding Questions

- State the goals and objectives of the lesson.
- Specify the main concepts to be taught.
- Frame the main concepts and guiding questions that students will answer and connect these to the essential questions of the unit.

Think About Students' Characteristics

Consider your students'

- prior knowledge
- cultural and socioeconomic background
- cognitive abilities

Prepare Guiding Questions to Use Throughout the Lesson

Develop questions that

- scaffold students' learning and address the needs of all learners
- include all three levels of questioning (literal, inferential, metacognitive)
- include sufficient variety to hold students' interest

Considering Goals, Objectives, and Essential Questions

The first step in planning questions is to decide the goals and objectives of the lesson and the reason for asking the questions. A question can be perfect in design and still not be appropriate. First, the question must have a clear content focus (Walsh & Sattes, 2005). This focus typically relates to the content specified by a grade-level curriculum—content that is usually determined by both state and national organizations. The teacher needs to identify the key concepts and pinpoint what students need to understand about them. Knowing the content's concepts and planning effective questions for a lesson is one domain that is now identified as a key area of the Annual Professional Performance Review (APPR).

Armed with this knowledge, the teacher should devise questions for the lesson. *Essential questions* are compelling questions that frame the unit of study and create the structure for the concepts that students will learn.

As an example, imagine that you are preparing a 3rd-grade unit based on the book *The Wednesday Surprise* by Eve Bunting (1989).This is a story in which a girl teaches her grandmother to read. The main concepts include the generations in a family, their typical roles, and the interesting things that happen when people reverse roles (in this case, when a young person teaches an adult to read). The essential questions for this unit, ones you hope the students will eventually be able to answer, may be these:

- Why is it important to understand the idea of generations?
- What is your evidence that people's roles have changed (or not changed) through the generations?
- Compare your life with your grandparents' lives. Which lifestyle do you prefer and why?

Similarly, for a 5th-grade unit on leadership, the teacher began the introduction by discussing the qualifications of teachers and students. His essential questions included the following:

- What are qualifications?
- How does one become qualified?
- Why is it important to be qualified for a job?
- What are the qualifications of a good teacher? What are the qualifications of good students?

In an 8th-grade class, the teacher was discussing integrity and scandals in connection to government officials. Her essential questions included:

- What is honor?
- What are elected officials' responsibilities to the community that they represent?
- What is a scandal?
- When does the public's value system impact an elected official?
- What can or should occur when there is a conflict between honor, responsibility, and public office?

Thinking About Students' Characteristics

Clearly, the students must have experiences with and knowledge about the concepts embedded in the questions you ask. This is true even for questions that might require students to hypothesize or imagine. Regardless of the type of question, there can be a match between the student and the question only if the student has had adequate preparation in the content. This is a central tenet in instruction. It means that the teacher understands what the question is asking the student to do cognitively, and what the student's level of development is in relationship to the contextual level of the question. Along with this, the teacher must be tuned in to the student's learning style and intelligence. The critical question the teacher must continually ask is: What is the match between the student and the question I am asking? We will discuss this more in later chapters.

For now, to ensure that there is a match between the question and the students' backgrounds and prior knowledge, teachers should ask *themselves* questions like these:

- What is their [the students'] understanding?
- What are their ideas?
- What do they feel?
- What do they believe? Value?
- What are their concerns? Interests? Questions?
- What do they want to do that involves changes?
- Who or what influences them? (Stevenson, 1986, p. 23)

To support students' growth and development, and to enhance the teacher's ability to plan for further instruction, questions posed in the classroom should represent a balance among content, concepts, thinking skills, and the children's knowledge. Figure 2.2 illustrates the components of cognition that are part of every task, including questions that students experience.

Figure 2.2. Cognitive Components in Students' Tasks

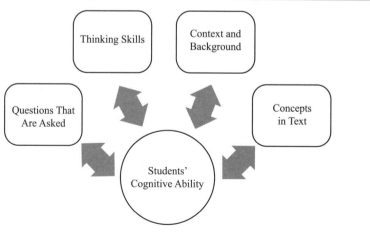

In many cases, students are ready to tackle a new concept if they have appropriate support. Such support can readily be made available through the Questioning Cycle. When a teacher carefully crafts questions around real concerns, relationships, and interests, students want to explore these issues and become more actively involved. For example, in lessons about *The Wednesday Surprise*, students were surprised to discover that some adults do not know how to read, and they enjoyed telling stories about times they helped adults. They also concluded that it was hard for them to teach adults, but that it was also fun. The story became an opportunity for the students to consider how and why we learn. Christopher, a child in this 3rd-grade class, discussed how he helped his grandmother learn how to send text messages with her cell phone. Other students had a number of similar experiences that they could share.

During this type of discussion, teachers are able to demonstrate that they are not looking for the "right" answer and that they are mainly interested in hearing about information that the child already has and the connections that he or she is making. It is an opportunity to build on creative ideas that come forward. Teachers can work toward having students identify with the questions and bring their experience to add to the topic. This process can be diagrammed as:

Teacher's questions → Student's reflection → Student's connections

Notice, in the next Questions in the Classroom, how 2nd-grader Jessica connects her background knowledge to the teacher's question and then, once she's comfortable with the process, goes on to add to the teacher's question.

Questions in the Classroom: Making Further Connections

TEACHER: The next chapter I will read to you is called "Cracked." Why might the author have used this title?

JESSICA: The submarine is having trouble.

TEACHER: What do you mean, "trouble"?

JESSICA: The octopus is holding the submarine.

TEACHER: So what does cracked have to do with this?

JESSICA: Maybe he is going to crack the submarine like you crack an egg.

TEACHER: What makes you think that?

JESSICA: I always think of Humpty Dumpty when I hear the word *cracked*.

TEACHER: Well, let's read and find out if in fact the submarine will be like Humpty.

JESSICA: And I want to add to your question: Will they be able to put the pieces back?

In this discussion, the teacher's response to Jessica invites her to focus on the use of the word *cracked*. The teacher is simultaneously working on the concept of *cracked* and asking about the purpose of chapter headings and what they do to assist reading comprehension. The questioning encourages Jessica to bring out her background knowledge and think beyond the text.

Another example of drawing out background knowledge comes from Jacqueline, a 5th-grade teacher, as she introduces a unit on the Holocaust. Jacqueline begins the lesson with the unit's essential question, "Why must we always remember the events of the Holocaust?" She poses the question to the entire class in order to focus students' attention on, and create an interest in, an even larger topic: "What impact can prejudice have on individuals, groups, and society?" During the discussion, she calls on volunteers but does not agree or disagree with each response. Instead, she records the responses and allows the students to make connections, provide evidence for their responses, and indicate how their ideas fit into the unit's essential question. That night, Jacqueline builds her questions for upcoming lessons out of the information that she has gathered in this session.

Crafting the Guiding Questions

The specific questions that the teacher asks during the lesson are often called *guiding questions*, because they guide the students' explorations. The guiding questions stem from the topic's essential questions, and their purpose is to form the structure that allows students to eventually answer the essential questions. Together, essential and guiding questions frame a discussion that can be lively and powerful, especially if the answers are not simple but have multiple perspectives and interpretations (Martin-Kniep, 2000).

Carefully crafted guiding questions produce a collaborative exchange that brings a quality and depth to learning. In an ideal world, a teacher plans a question and then goes through a series of follow-up questions with the student. Peers may be called upon to participate in the interaction depending upon the flow of the conversation. When teachers ask these questions, they generally begin by defining the concept and building the students' related content vocabulary. As the teacher asks related follow-up questions, students are required to refine their thinking and be critical, creative participants. If we go back to the example of *The Wednesday Surprise*, an early part of the questioning and discussion might look like this:

1. Defining the concept being taught:
    What is a generation? (The students give the main characteristics of the term *generation*.)
2. Elaborating on the characteristics:
    Why are these characteristics important? (One student presents an opinion.)
3. Providing evidence for the student's thinking:
    How do you know this? (The student provides evidence for his/her thinking about generations and communities.)
4. Creating generalizations and conclusions:
    Why is it important to understand the contributions of each generation? (The student begins to draw conclusions or generalizations regarding generations.)

Thus, the steps in the discussion move in a sequential fashion from literal, defining characteristics to those that are elaborated and/or inferred, and the discussion moves toward the recognition of multiple student perspectives about what a generation is. The purpose is to have students consistently create ideas, decide which ideas are important, ask questions of their own, and justify their knowledge. You can see, too, that the questions build toward the lesson's essential questions that the teacher defined earlier.

Some teachers use a graphic organizer to help students construct their understanding of concepts being discussed during the Questioning Cycle. This device reinforces the concept, expands vocabulary, and provides students with visual information that they can refer to when elaborating on the concept. Figure 2.3 is an example of a graphic organizer.

When a teacher plans guiding questions in this way, the questions not only facilitate the development of the concepts of the lesson, but also allow the teacher to:

1. Interactively review previously learned materials
    Example: Students have completed work with materials on the solar system, and the teacher wants to review what they have learned. The teacher may ask, "How many planets are there in our solar system?"
2. Connect and/or compare information in different areas
    Example: The teacher asks, "How would you compare the characters in Kate DiCamillo's books?"

3. Consider contradictions
    Example: The teacher asks, "In Chris Van Allsberg's (1986)
        book *The Stranger*, why does the author create so many
        contradictions in his story?"

Scaffolding Questions

In addition to encouraging students to think and interact with the
ideas of their peers, guiding questions should scaffold the students' learning. Scaffolding, in this case, means creating supports that gradually expand the knowledge within the learner. Appropriate scaffolding in the

Figure 2.3. Sample Graphic Organizer for the Lesson on Generations

CONCEPT: GENERATIONS	
Main Characteristics of the Term	Words That Relate to the Topic of Generations
Examples and Non-Examples of Generations	Description or Drawing of Generations

guiding questions allows students to construct their knowledge, build their schema related to the concept, and comprehend the depth of the topic's essential questions. In my many years of observing teachers, I have realized that good teachers do this sort of scaffolding all day long. They provide a strong base and structure for the concept being taught. Then they gradually remove the structure as the students develop their ability to apply the information. In *The Wednesday Surprise* lesson, the teacher might use guiding questions like these as part of the scaffolding process:

What is a role reversal?
What could I teach my parents or grandparents?

Such questions would gradually build students' understanding of the story and its implications. If the teacher realized that students had limited knowledge of immigrant grandparents, this concept would also need to be developed further.

Careful scaffolding, based on an assessment of the students' background knowledge, allows the teacher to include students of all abilities in the discussion. The teacher can differentiate instruction through the questions and thereby meet the different needs of the various students. The purpose is for the guiding questions to support *all* students in being able to answer the essential questions of the unit. This type of structure supports the students at different learning levels and increases the chance that all learners will move ahead. Although the preplanning initially takes time, the results are that more students participate and engage in the learning.

Often, this is a very different questioning routine from what students have experienced. Most often, they expect the teacher to say the answer is "right" and then to move to the next question with no further elaboration. I have found that even graduate students have the same expectation. It takes most students time to get used the idea of "building" or scaffolding a perspective, and to appreciate that responses can be diverse, not simply right or wrong. It also takes time for them to be comfortable with the idea that the teacher is going to ask the question a number of times until all students' responses have been exhausted.

Students better understand the procedure when the guiding questions are authentic ones that make clear connections to the unit of study. Here are some further examples:

1. We have been talking about clothes and the use of buttons and zippers. How are these useful, and why are they sometimes a problem?
2. What impact does the weather forecast have on us?

3. The president has been speaking about borders. What are they, and why is this an important issue?
4. Jessica just asked, "What is a dimension?" Who can explain this to us?
5. We have been discussing polynomials, binomials, and trinomials. How would you compare and contrast them?

Questions like these are often successful with students because they are useful, meaningful, and consistent with their experiential background, yet still attend to the central focus of the lesson. I also recommend that teachers post their essential questions in the classroom to remind students of the unit's focus and to assist students in discussing how the lesson's guiding questions fit into the essential questions. Highlighting the questions in this way encourages students to:

1. focus their attention on important concepts in the lesson;
2. relate information in a text to the most appropriate set of background experiences;
3. create a coherent framework for understanding and remembering the concepts; and
4. practice cognitive skills that they will ultimately be able to use on their own (Pearson, 1982).

Structuring Questions

As part of the scaffolding process, teachers should plan an appropriate mix of the three levels of questions discussed in Chapter 1: literal, inferential, and metacognitive. For the lesson based on *The Wednesday Surprise*, the teacher might plan questions such as these:

Where does the story take place? (literal)
Why are the location and time important in this story? (inferential)
Explain the family structure and how generations are present in this story. (literal)
How did the grandmother learn to read? Why was it important for the grandmother to learn to read? How did the grandmother's being an immigrant influence her inability to read? (literal)
Why is this story about role reversal? (inferential)
Have you ever taught your parents or grandparents something? What was the experience like for you? (literal)
What does this story tell us about Anna's relationship with her grandmother? What are some ways that we could contribute to other people who are like our grandparents? (inferential)

What did Anna actually accomplish? (inferential)
How did you learn to read? Why was it important for you?
　　(metacognitive)

Sometimes even our literal questions can lead to interesting discussions and new avenues in classrooms where discussions are the norm. Notice in the following example how the teacher's initial, literal question encourages these 1st-grade students to wonder about peanuts. The teacher follows up with further questions that are both literal and inferential.

Questions in the Classroom: Discovery

TEACHER: Yesterday you found it interesting when you opened the peanut shells and found that they were different inside. When you opened the peanut shells, what did you find?

TRICIA: I found two peanuts.

SHUJUAN: I found four peanuts.

TEACHER: How many did you find in your peanut?

CRISTIN: None.

TEACHER: You were surprised. Why?

CRISTIN: I wanted a peanut in mine.

TEACHER: What do you think happened to it?

CRISTIN: Maybe an ant got in there and ate it.

TEACHER: Why do you think that? What evidence do you have?

CRISTIN: Ants are small and peanuts are small, and ants get into lots of things in my house.

TEACHER: Does anyone else have any ideas about what happened to her peanut?

CARA: Maybe somebody cracked it open, ate it and taped it back together again.

TEACHER: Let's check on that. Was there any tape on your peanut?

CRISTIN: No, it was all closed up and hard to open.

TEACHER: Other ideas?

RUBY: Maybe it was microscopic and she didn't see the tiny bit and it fell on the floor when she was trying to open it and she didn't see the microscopic piece.

TEACHER: That's another idea. What else?

HEIDI: Maybe it just didn't grow at all. I have had that happen to me at Sheriff Joe's. They give you peanuts when you wait for your dinner, and I have opened some that did not have a peanut in them. Maybe they just don't have enough to grow a shell and a nut.

CRISTIN: I think that is a good idea because all people don't grow
evenly. Maybe peanuts don't grow perfectly all the time.
TEACHER: What are some ways we can check to see why there wasn't a
peanut in the shell?

It is obvious that learning is flourishing here. Students learn to elaborate on the questions, and they build on one another's ideas. As students become more engaged in the questioning process, teachers also feel a sense of accomplishment and ease with the divergent ideas that emerge.

PUTTING IT INTO A LESSON

Let's look at a lesson plan and then consider how a teacher might think through the concepts and different levels of questions. Figure 2.4 explores these levels in a 2nd-grade lesson.

Lesson Plan: Grade 2 Language Arts
Reading Standards: Students will describe how words and phrases
supply rhythm and meaning in a story.
Essential Question: What are idiomatic expressions?
Guiding Questions: How does Peggy Parish use idiomatic expressions
her story *Amelia Bedelia*?
Performance Objectives: Students will be able to:

- identify idiomatic expressions
- compare the literal meaning and hidden meaning in an idiomatic
  expression

Concepts: Idiomatic expressions
Skills: Students will be able to use idiomatic expressions in their writing.
Materials: Students will listen to the story *Amelia Bedelia*.

PLANNING AND FLEXIBILITY

A key point to remember is that while the teacher plans a number of questions, the lesson may proceed in such a way that all the questions may not need to be asked. Sometimes the key ideas come out as students are elaborating on their thoughts. As teachers, we need to remember to be flexible. Planning, in fact, increases your flexibility because once you have a plan, you can listen more attentively and be ready to change direction when students generate ideas that you did not expect.

Figure 2.4. Different Levels of Questions

Essential Questions	Guiding Questions	Background Knowledge	Thinking Level
What is an idiomatic expression?	How do idioms add to this story?	What do you know about *Amelia Bedelia*?	Students must be able to define idioms. This involves literal thinking.
How do we identify an idiom?	Which idiom did you like in the story? Why?	Why do people like to read *Amelia Bedelia?* How do the idioms influence the story?	Ascertaining the impact of idioms on a story requires inferential thinking: Students apply conceptual knowledge to story structure.
What happens when a word has more than one meaning?	Which words have more than one meaning?	Words can have more than one meaning.	Recognition that one word can represent more than one idea is inferential thinking and requires interpretation.
What is an author's purpose in using an idiom?	Find an idiomatic expression in the story. What is the purpose of idioms in this story?	How does an author's style impact a story?	Evaluating the author's style and use of idioms as a literary method requires inferential thinking, analysis, and judgment.

In the next Questions in the Classroom, notice how the teacher guides the discussion in this 2nd-grade classroom but steps back and allows for wider student participation to extend the ideas. Some of the questions were planned, but others arose spontaneously as the teacher responded to the students.

Questions in the Classroom: Flexibility

TEACHER: We have been reading and researching about wild weather. We will actually be able to see some examples of the wild weather we have been discussing.

OLIVIA: I have a book on wild weather, too. I am going to use that for my research.

TEACHER: That's fine. But before we do our experiments, let's review some research and reading we have done on tornadoes. What have we learned so far?

SAMUEL: Most tornadoes occur between April, May, and June. That's when the cold air meets the warm air near the Earth's surface.

TEACHER: Can you explain what happens?

SAMUEL: We have a thunderstorm and then sometimes a tornado.

TEACHER: Would you elaborate on your answer, or would anyone like to build on this?

NICHOLAS: The cold air pushes under the warm air. The warm air is lighter than the cold air and it rises fast. Then the warm air moves upward and makes a tornado.

SAMUEL: The warm air is lighter and wet so it goes up and rises and spins. It then twists around.

NICHOLAS: That's why tornadoes are sometimes called twisters— because they twist around.

ADRIANA: I read that some people call them cyclones, and they have wind speeds that can be over 300 miles an hour. I knew they were fast but not that fast, and I learned that no other wind blows faster. But they don't last long.

MELODY: Don't some tornadoes come out of the water?

TEACHER: From your different readings, can anyone answer that?

OLIVIA: In my book, it showed tornadoes on the water.

TEACHER: And what did you learn from that source?

OLIVIA: I don't know but I will look in my book.

BURT: I read about waterspouts, and they are tornadoes that go across the water at high speeds. I think that waterspouts are tornadoes that start on the water because my book had a picture of one. Like tornadoes, they pick up things because of their speed.

TEACHER: What do you mean they pick up things?

BURT: Because they are spinning so fast they knock over stuff, and it gets picked up in the air. Tornadoes can pick up little stuff like a garbage pail or big stuff like a train.

ARIELLE: No! I saw a movie and the tornadoes picked up trucks, but a train is huge.

TEACHER: Well, let's continue our research and see what else we can find out about what they can pick up. Does anyone else want to add to this discussion?

SAMUEL: Where do tornadoes go when a tornado is over?

TEACHER: Does anyone want to answer that question?

HOWARD: If tornadoes happen because the warm and cold air meet and the winds are blowing, maybe the temperatures even out and the tornado stops. Or, maybe it stops because the rain stops.

NICOLAS: If it stops, what happens to all the stuff it has picked up along the way? Does it just all drop out of the sky?

TEACHER: We have a lot of unanswered questions. Let's make a list of the types of wild weather storms and then move to our computers and books and see if we can come up with the answers to these questions and descriptions of the different types of storms.

EFFECTIVE QUESTIONS

What we have seen in this chapter is that good lesson planning is the key to good questions and instructional practice. The teacher builds the lesson starting with an awareness of how the lesson fits into the overall unit. From the goals and objectives, the teacher frames the essential questions that structure the class' exploration of the topic. Next, the teacher thinks about the students' prior knowledge, background, cognitive abilities, and the support that may be needed to help students reach the desired objectives. Finally, the teacher plans guiding questions to direct the discussion and extend students' thinking. Figure 2.5 illustrates this process.

As a principal, when I was meeting with a teacher in a pre-conference meeting prior to a classroom observation, I would always review with the teacher the lesson's guiding questions so that we were both focused on the main ideas of the lesson. There are many benefits that occur when teachers plan the lesson to use effective questioning techniques. The shift toward a more interactive, respectful environment becomes apparent because everyone is used to listening carefully to one another.

Unfortunately, mentors cannot be available on a daily basis to support teachers. But teachers can become their own coaches. They can ask themselves a series of questions that will keep them on track with the questions and concepts they have planned for the lesson:

Figure 2.5. Goals and Objectives of the Content and Lesson

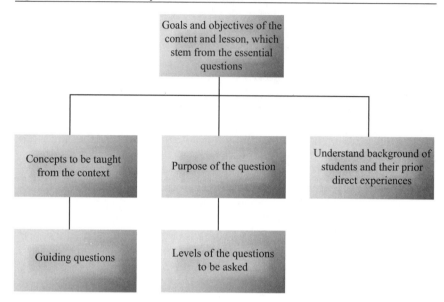

As a teacher, do I:

1. serve as a guide and facilitator, rather than a dispenser of information?
2. see that students actively construct their knowledge?
3. notice the development of language, vocabulary, and conversation as students articulate their thoughts?
4. build students' content and social knowledge by scaffolding information?
5. help students develop an appreciation for alternative points of view?
6. assess the students' responses and knowledge?
7. foster decision-making as students consider the merits of their peers' responses?
8. help students clarify ideas and resolve problems?
9. encourage diversity and involvement in the classroom?

I also encourage teachers to tape different lessons to use as a professional development opportunity. Tapes help teachers hear what is actually happening in the lesson so that they can revisit the goals of their lessons to determine their areas of strength. They also can hear the effectiveness of the questions they have planned and can decide how well they met their lesson objectives. This type of reflective practice supports best practice, allowing the teachers to consider and adjust their instruction.

Teacher Reflection: Listening to Students

How surprised I was to listen to my tape. First, my monotone voice was very upsetting to me. But what really upset me the most was listening to my voice finishing the students' answers. I never realized that I don't give them a chance to finish their answers. If I think the answer is what I want, I just finish their sentence and give the rest of the answer. Boy, do I have a lot to learn about questioning and helping my students grow in their language and thinking. Taping is a safe way for me to improve my effectiveness. While the first tape was hard for me, I will do it more so I can keep improving.

—3rd-grade teacher

Action Items

1. Several times, and in different situations, place a tape recorder in your classroom and tape your questioning of students. Listen to the questions and student responses. Ask yourself, "What effect did my questions have on students' learning?"
2. After a lesson in which you have used a series of planned and varied questions and then listened to responses, ask the students to reflect on the lesson and give you feedback on the Questioning Cycle. You can also listen with a peer and review the questions and responses.
3. Think back to a lesson you taught today. What guiding question might you have planned and then asked that would have connected to the essential questions of your unit? What changes might have occurred if you had started with planned guiding questions?

CHAPTER THREE

Structuring the Question

What is a question, you ask? Everything. It is the way of evoking stimulating response or stultifying inquiry. It is, in essence, the very core of teaching.

—John Dewey

In discussing question planning, Chapter 2 suggested that the guiding questions in a lesson should be structured to scaffold the students' learning and to include all three types of questions (literal, inferential, and meta-cognitive). Before we leave the planning stage in the Questioning Cycle, we should explore the structure of questions more deeply, considering their function in the lesson and their role in developing the students' cognitive abilities. What follows is a brief introduction to those approaches that I feel are most helpful. I include them to broaden your background knowledge and to provide you with choices, because one system does not fit all teachers.

APPROACHES TO STRUCTURING QUESTIONS

Personally, I have found that the best approach is one based on Bloom's Taxonomy, but I suggest that readers experiment with various approaches and then decide which best fits their teaching style. I have even observed teachers using different systems at different times, choosing the one that most appropriately matched what was being taught. Selecting and learning to use these methods does take time. It took me 2 years to completely integrate this process into my teaching, but I have seen other teachers make the shift in only a few months.

As we explore methods for structuring questions and for differentiating instruction to fit students' learning styles, it is crucial for teachers to remember that their questions should not feel like a quiz. Rather, the teacher should envision questions as a frame to maintain the focus of the lesson, and expect that students' own questions will be—and should be—part of the ongoing conversation. This is a time when the teacher will also

be encouraging students to share their opinions so that a sense of em-
powerment is built. Based on the knowledge that is being constructed,
a student may ask a question that will itself shift a discussion (King &
Rosenshine, 1993). But the key is that teachers need to carefully design
their questions, monitor them, and be willing to revise these as the lesson
progresses. Carefully constructed questions provide students with an environment that is broad in nature and that gives them the opportunity to
apply their growing knowledge across disciplines. According to J. T. Dillon, this type of broad thinking occurs when teachers ask themselves two
questions when planning questions:

1. What is it that students are to learn from this lesson?
2. To which questions does that knowledge or learning represent
   an answer?

When this occurs, teachers can accomplish more than just getting responses
to their questions (Dillon, 1990). Teachers must observe the unfolding lesson and react to the responses of the students, which involves preplanning
the questions and revising along the way. This process helps to maintain the
big ideas and larger context of the lesson.

In his 2005 monograph, *Asking Effective Questions*, Lawrence F. Lowery
from the University of California, Berkeley, formulates an approach that
encourages teachers to ask effective questions. His work aims to connect
the learner, instruction, and content, and he recommends assessing students' intellectual growth by creating activities that match their development. Lowery elaborates the structure of literal and inferential questions,
and also suggests that teachers can ask questions directly or in the form of
a statement that accomplishes the same thing. (An example of a "question
statement" might be: Tell me what has happened to your seed.) Lowery
has also created a structure that illustrates different categories of questions
that teachers can readily use to keep track of their questioning (see Figure
3.1). He believes, as I do, that teachers' questioning improves when the
teacher consistently monitors his or her questioning strategies in the classroom by either keeping a journal/workbook or by taping (audio or visual).

The categories of questions that Lowery (2005) presents are:

1. *Confirming questions:* Ask students to remember information,
   such as a specific name of something, a part of a definition, or a
   recalled fact.
2. *Integrating questions:* Ask a student to analyze and arrive at a
   particular idea or to develop particular ideas in his or her own
   terms. Clues may or may not be given.

Figure 3.1. Questions and Question Statements

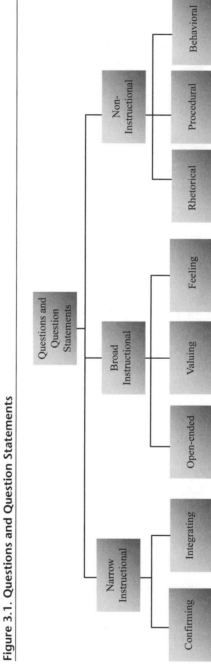

3. *Open-ended questions:* Encourage students to freely explore, analyze, and synthesize information related to a topic or problem. Clues may sometimes be given. As students explore their thinking, they come up with novel ideas and solutions. A variety of divergent responses are expected.
4. *Valuing questions:* Ask students to synthesize information to develop an opinion, judgment, or evaluation. Students then state a preference.
5. *Feeling questions:* Ask students to describe a feeling or express an emotion. The teacher expects a variety of answers.
6. *Rhetorical questions:* No answer is expected.
7. *Procedural questions:* Deal with classroom management, not with the content of a lesson.
8. *Behavioral questions:* Used to control behavior in the lesson.

Lowery believes that encouraging teachers to keep track of their questions will help them to improve their skill in structuring and employing the questions, as well as provide a more complete understanding of what is really being accomplished cognitively. Lowery has a chart in his book that illustrates a method for maintaining a log of questions. In a like manner, in a graduate class that I teach, students tape their lessons and then analyze them later to determine the cognitive levels of their questions and the responses of their students. In particular, they look at (or listen to) how well they follow up each question, and whether they are promoting a discussion in which concepts can be fully developed. It has been my experience that teachers learn a great deal by doing this. Taking the time to analyze their question provides teachers with unfettered, truthful feedback about their effectiveness.

BLOOM'S TAXONOMY

A commonly used approach is one based on Bloom's *Taxonomy of Educational Objectives* (1987), which comprises six major cognitive categories along with five affective categories. The categories are arranged as a hierarchy, which some critics have objected to because they believe that there is no hierarchy of thought. In reality, however, the categories overlap within the students' mental processing. The information a student has about a concept is connected within his/her mental schema, and thus, the response given reflects what information the student has or feels should be given. Students respond to the question they think has been asked and qualify their response based on the relationship with the teacher and the content.

Teacher Reflection: Flexible Questioning

I had several benefits from working on questioning and taping my lessons. I finally can listen to my tapes without feeling uncomfortable. I just don't like my voice on tape. I hear others complaining about how their voices sound so I guess I am not alone. Taping has made me think about my voice and how I use it when speaking to my students. I never begin a lesson without my focus question, which will help my students' growth intellectually. I plan the rest of my questions but I don't have to use them all. I can stray when the discussion goes in an important direction. I keep a sheet with students' names next to me and use a check system to tell me about the level of their responses. It isn't exactly what you showed us or what we have read about but it definitely works for me.

—8th-grade teacher

Originally, Bloom's Taxonomy was intended to describe both the cognitive and affective aspects of learning. It was written by a committee of college and university examiners because the university communities (University of Chicago, Duke University, University of Arkansas, Michigan State University, and Syracuse University) believed that materials and exams could be better shared across disciplines and universities if there were a framework for rating the materials and tests. Bloom and the committee created a hierarchical series of categories that have since been used for writing cognitive objectives and questions. The six categories are shown a little later on in Figure 3.2 and were established to apply to both oral and written questions. By using these categories, the committees believed teachers would become aware of the cognitive level of their questions and direct them toward analysis and interpretation questions.

Many studies across several disciplines (including reading, science, and social studies) have examined the efficacy of this approach, and they consistently demonstrate that most teachers employ questions that rely on memory (and are thus low-level cognitive activities). These findings emphasize the need for teachers to practice using the different levels if they hope to encourage critical and divergent thinking.

Bloom's categories create a manageable questioning system and provide a strategy for constructing questions that encourages teachers to move from the literal level to the inferential level of thinking. Appendix A contains a condensed version of the *Taxonomy of Educational Objectives*;

however, for our purposes, I will only explore the six cognitive domain categories.

Each category is comprised of a series of verbs so that teachers can write the objectives for their lessons and then tie the questions they plan to ask to what they hope to accomplish in the lessons. The distinction between the literal and abstract is also described so that as teachers are guided by these verbs, they see that a question might require a simple or a more complex mental activity. For example, a teacher would know that asking a student to name a river requires simpler thinking behavior than asking a student to describe how a river might benefit a community. Figure 3.2 is a diagram of Bloom's categories, which can be used as an organizing structure for asking diverse questions. The related verbs for each of the categories appears next.

Taxonomy Verbs and Levels

Literal level

- *Knowledge:* recall, define, state, name, recognize, explain, list, describe, predict, select, tell, read, determine, identify, label, organize, study, classify, and conduct

Literal and transitional level

- *Comprehension:* explain, understand, translate, reorder, interpret, discuss, describe, prepare, explain the significance of, relate, distinguish, draw conclusions, deal with conclusions, estimate, differentiate, classify, construct, illustrate, represent, select, and report

Abstract level

- *Application:* apply, discuss, identify, solve, determine, predict, explore, explain, change, classify, experiment, relate, adapt, modify, figure out, conclude, persuade, and conduct
- *Analysis:* analyze, break down, detect, express, label, recognize, compose, examine, distinguish, detect, recognize cause and effect, recognize unstated assumptions, infer, investigate, state consequences, draw conclusions, make assumptions, construct, consider, and compare
- *Synthesis:* synthesize, think, integrate, draw out, respond, persuade, propose, plan, build, change, consider, hypothesize,

Figure 3.2. Bloom's Taxonomy for Objectives and Questions

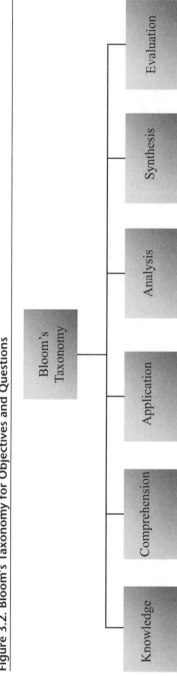

represent, deduct, distinguish, propose, combine, reorganize, write, create, invent, design, formulate, perceive, interpret, debate, and defend

- *Evaluation:* evaluate, judge, test, weigh, appraise, determine criteria, value, state opinion, decide, indicate fallacies, choose, debate, defend, criticize, and justify

Using the Taxonomy to Structure Questions

The most important reason for using Bloom's Taxonomy is to help prepare a range of diverse cognitive questions that will:

- establish students' level of basic knowledge, and
- bridge the literal and inferential levels of thinking to enhance the intellectual abilities of students.

It has been successfully demonstrated that Bloom's Taxonomy improves students' ability to respond to high-level questions (Stabile, 2001).

Note that some of the verbs I just listed are found in more than one category because they can be used either literally or inferentially. For example, "explain" and "distinguish" are found at both the literal and the abstract level because the nature of the task depends upon the question asked. This point illustrates two elements of the process that teachers need to understand: First, teachers need to be clear about the purpose of each question and the level of response they expect or hope to elicit; second, they must recognize that the bridge between literal and inferential levels of thinking builds cognitive development.

Here is an example of the use of Bloom's Taxonomy to structure questions in a lesson about the solar system and space exploration:

1. What planet is nearest the sun? (knowledge)
2. How does the sun help the Earth? (comprehension)
3. How would you build a better spaceship? (application)
4. We have been discussing spaceships. What might NASA do to improve their designs? (analysis)
5. In the article "Safety and Space Exploration," what do you think is the author's theme or purpose for writing the article? (synthesis)
6. Evaluate the author's style of writing in this article. (evaluation)
7. What has been the most interesting part of this unit of study for you? (analysis)
8. Analyze the impact of outsourcing. (analysis)

9. Prepare an alternate to the current geometric design for this project. (synthesis)
10. Assess the impact of the current environmental situation in cities in China based on your knowledge of the global energy cycle. (evaluation)

Extending Bloom's Taxonomy

Several authors have built on Bloom's Taxonomy. The book *Stating Objectives for Classroom Instruction* (Gronlund, 1985) is a practical guide that reviews and summarizes Bloom's work and also creates a list of additional verbs for the cognitive and affective domains that teachers can use to prepare their objective and questions (see Appendix B). It is interesting to compare Gronlund's list with Bloom's Taxonomy. As teachers use either or both of these lists, they can add their own verbs to extend the range of their questions. Another interesting elaboration of Bloom's Taxonomy can be found in *The New Taxonomy of Educational Objectives* (Marzano & Kendall, 2007). This book describes each of the levels and connects them to the different content areas.

Still another model, based on revisions of Bloom (with a hint of Lowery's earlier works), is the one proposed by Anderson and Krathwohl (2001), who use the cognitive categories of Bloom and suggest that questions should explore factual, conceptual, procedural, and metacognitive knowledge. This model is interesting because it allows teachers to simultaneously consider the knowledge (concepts of the lesson) and the students' cognitive processes (thinking skills as connected to the lesson objectives) when preparing questions. It also encourages teachers to focus on those concepts and skills that need development and determine how these connect to the content of the lesson. Figure 3.3 is a representation of

---

Teacher Reflection: Student Engagement

I've posted Bloom's verbs on the wall in my room, and I am beginning to see a light. Students are more engaged when I use better questions. Students are more engaged when I use inferential questions. Even the students who don't necessarily understand all of what is being said pay more attention. I think they feel the other students' interest in what is being said. How long does it take to really be able to master this process?

—7th-grade teacher

this model, and I have found that teachers like this format for designing and keeping track of their questions. It also reminds them to simultaneously think about the distinctions in their questions and to note the knowledge (factual, conceptual, procedural, or metacognitive) and the cognitive nature of the question. These distinctions remind teachers to move from literal to inferential questions. For these reasons, this model is extremely helpful in building lesson designs and curriculum mapping.

Figure 3.3. The Cognitive Process Dimension

The Knowledge Dimension	The Cognitive Process Dimension					
	1 *Remember*	*2* *Understand*	*3* *Apply*	*4* *Analyze*	*5* *Evaluate*	*6* *Create*
A. Factual Knowledge						
B. Conceptual Knowledge						
C. Procedural Knowledge						
D. Metacognitive Knowledge						

THE COSTA MODEL

The last model to be considered here is the one proposed by Art Costa, who has had a great impact on teaching for thinking. Costa (2001) suggests that there are four types of questions that teachers can ask:

- *Clarifying questions:* These questions prompt a student to elaborate on his or her responses because the teacher is not sure of what the student means. The teacher may say, "Tell me more about that."
- *Cuing questions:* These provide clues as to the direction or purpose of the questions. For example, "What benefits have we had from exploring space?"
- *Focus questions:* These focus the inquiry to obtain more precise and detailed information from students. For example, "What are the specific characteristics of that planet that make life possible there?"
- *Probing questions:* These questions seek more information and extend the thinking of the students. For example, "Why do you think that?"

Once again, these four types of questions assist teachers in moving from the literal level to the inferential level of thinking. This method is another way for teachers to plan their questions for a lesson and to reap the benefits of a shared discussion.

DIFFERENTIATED INSTRUCTION

Whatever technique or method a teacher selects for devising questioning strategies, he or she has to tailor the instruction to the aptitudes, specific needs, skills, and preferences of the students. Look back at Figure 2.1 to refresh your memory on the importance of students' characteristics in the question-planning process.

Several authors capably describe differentiated instruction, notably Keirsey and Bates (1978), Gardner (1991), and Tomlinson (1999). Each of these thinkers advocates the necessity of acknowledging that students think and perform differently. Gardner (2006), for example, has described several different forms of what he calls multiple intelligences that underlie learning processes:

- Linguistic intelligence
- Visual-spatial intelligence
- Musical intelligence
- Bodily-kinesthetic intelligence
- Intrapersonal intelligence
- Interpersonal intelligence
- Logical-mathematical intelligence
- Naturalist intelligence

The naturalist intelligence was added to the first seven intelligences later in his work.

These types of intelligence are not mutually exclusive, and every person can possess them in different degrees. But if you keep Gardner's forms of intelligence in mind when structuring questions, you will know, for example, that a summary question will appeal to students who tend to use linguistic intelligence, a question that asks students to "illustrate" will appeal to visual-spatial students, and a question that calls for judgment will appeal to logical-mathematical learners.

The two fundamental tenets of differentiated instruction are that individuals differ in their preferences and intellectual processing and that teachers need to respect and creatively deal with these differences. Carol

Ann Tomlinson's extensive writing helps broaden our perspective on these matters. Like her predecessors (Dewey, 1991; Kamii, Manning, & Manning, 1991; Piaget, 1974), Tomlinson and McTighe underscore the important principle that learning occurs in an individual manner for each student. In their recent book, *Integrating Differentiated Instruction and Understanding by Design: Connecting Content and Kids* (2006), they expand this belief and incorporate into her suggested lesson and curriculum designs the idea that learning occurs not *at* the individual level or *to* the individual but *within* the individual students as they are engaged in the process of exploring the concepts. McTighe and Wiggins (1999) describe this process as identifying the enduring understandings. Teachers who are committed to their diverse students can read the writing of Thomas Armstrong in his book *Multiple Intelligences* (1994). The book contains a chart that illustrates questions a teacher might ask students that match their ability, preference, and level of thinking according to Bloom and Gardner. This further helps teachers with the process of differentiating their instruction. "Teachers can articulate competencies that address all seven intelligences as well Bloom's six levels of cognitive complexity" in their teaching (Armstrong, 1994, p. 154). The teacher can build in diversity by employing a number of cognitive levels and intelligences by using the types of questions that Armstrong uses.

Further, this approach is based on the idea that learners *construct* knowledge. Students must be actively engaged and responsible for their learning, which they must be able to connect to their background experience. My colleague Jacqueline Grennon Brooks (2002) has written: "Constructivism states that learners approach new experiences with a set of pre-established beliefs and naive theories. Learners change those beliefs and theories only when they cannot reconcile new data with presently held conceptions" (p. 130). In order to differentiate instruction, teachers must continually assess the thinking of their students to understand what concepts need to be more fully explored.

As a strategy, the Questioning Cycle works in concert with differentiated instruction. *Learning begins not with the content or text but with questions that students respond to.* Teachers differentiate the content by their planned questions, the process by asking different types of questions, and the end result by accepting different responses from students, and they then follow up with feedback to add to the answer.

Appreciating differences is so often talked about, but demonstrating what this means in a classroom is a different story. It takes time and the investigation of a variety of theories and philosophical orientations before a teacher really understands that most children in the class do not learn in the same manner that the teacher does (Myers, 1985). Therefore, there is a need for a vast variety of teaching techniques to be infused into the program to meet all the different learning strengths of the students. It is important that teachers let students in on their thinking about the strategies and their own style and preference for learning. Students need to know that all of these techniques may not fit their preferences but that they need to select from among and between techniques to help them when they are responding. Students need to tell about their preferences for learning and what techniques work for them.

In working with teachers, we have created the following questions for teachers to ask themselves at the planning stage. This type of informal assessment is helpful in planning the guiding questions for the lesson.

1. What learning preference does a student display?
2. Does a student answer certain types of questions regularly?
3. Are there types of questions that a student hesitates to answer because of his or her own learning preferences?
4. Do verbal students prefer answering questions that encourage interviews, debates, or critiques?
5. Do these same students shy away from activities that require measurement, diagramming, and designing?

TIPS FOR BEGINNING THE PROCESS

The match between the student, the content, and the question is individualized and complicated, and it takes time for a teacher to be able to balance all of these components. I suggest beginning with Bloom's Taxonomy and then systematically building from that baseline to include differentiation and student preferences.

For teachers who are new to questioning strategies, the easiest kind of lesson to plan is one in which the class discusses a book or newspaper article. For example, Mrs. Carmen, a 2nd-grade teacher, decided to read Bernard Waber's *Ira Sleeps Over* (1972) with her class in order to discuss the concepts of fear and peer pressure and to review the idea of friendship in a story. Here are the sequences of questions she used, moving from literal to abstract thinking and connecting to Gardner's multiple intelligences.

Questions in the Classroom: A Starter Lesson

Mrs. Carmen's class is reading *Ira Sleeps Over*, and the teacher has organized the questions in categories: sleepovers, friendship, fears.

Questions About Sleepovers:

- Tell about the first time you slept over at a friend's house. (knowledge, linguistic intelligence)
- Describe the feeling that you had. (comprehension, linguistic intelligence)
- How did Ira feel about sleeping at Reggie's house? (knowledge, analysis, interpersonal intelligence)
- Tell ways that a sleepover you had was similar to or different from Ira's sleepover. (analysis, logical-mathematical intelligence)

Questions About Friendship:

- Describe Ira. (knowledge, linguistic intelligence)
- Describe Reggie. (knowledge, linguistic intelligence)
- Explain why the boys are friends. (comprehension, application, linguistic intelligence)

Questions About Fears:

- How do you feel about sleeping in the dark? (knowledge, intrapersonal intelligence)
- Why do you think you have these feelings about the dark? (analysis, visual-spatial intelligence)
- Was it all right for Ira to want to bring his teddy bear? Why? (comprehension, interpersonal intelligence)
- Suppose Reggie had told Ira he slept with a teddy bear. What might have happened? (application, interpersonal intelligence)
- Why did Ira change his mind about taking his teddy bear to Reggie's house? (comprehension, linguistic intelligence)
- Contrast this with what you would have done. (analysis, intrapersonal intelligence)

Mrs. Carmen then used differentiated instructional activities to follow up on the questions. She created three activities:

- Write a paragraph telling what you liked about the story. (comprehension, intrapersonal intelligence)
- Who would like to do some writing about our story? (Select someone in the class who then writes and acts out Ira's comments to Reggie in the morning.) (application, bodily-kinesthetic intelligence)

- Create a series of questions that we can send to Bernard Waber.
- What questions might you want to ask him? Why would you ask these questions? (synthesis, interpersonal intelligence)

Keep in mind that although Mrs. Carmen planned all these questions, the students' responses actually guided the direction of subsequent questions. The responses revealed which areas need to be probed and extended. You might not ask all of your questions, but you need a preconceived plan to think through the major content of the story and to guide the discussion.

VARIETY IN QUESTIONING

This chapter has presented several approaches for creating questions that build students' cognitive abilities. Whichever approach you choose, I encourage you to monitor your questions to ensure that you use a range of different types of questions. By continually varying the types of questions you ask, you not only enable students to reach more complex levels of thinking, but you also prevent boredom and disengagement. Remember that unexpected or sophisticated questioning can revitalize the students' curiosity and participation.

For example, most students expect teachers to begin reading a book with a prediction question: "Look at the cover. What you think this story will be about?" A variant on this question might be, "Look at this book's cover and think about its title. What other book or story does this remind you of? Can you connect it to something else we have read?" A teacher might also ask the students why a particular book is being read that day. With this kind of diversity, we can reach different learners, enhance different concepts, and build inferential thinking.

When I am preparing a lesson, I always keep next to me a sheet listing different types of questions that I can ask (examples follow and there is a modified version in Appendix C). I encourage teachers to post this list or Bloom's Taxonomy in their classroom so that it is continually visible. I don't necessarily use all of these kinds of questions in a lesson, but they help me guide the discussion without asking the same types of questions over and over.

- Compare and contrast
- Clarification
- Change
- Point of view
- Feelings

- Preferences
- Summary
- Evaluation
- Consequences
- Relational

Or I may use the following questions to facilitate the discussion.

- What hypothetical question could you create?
- What do you anticipate this might be about?
- What would you plan to do as a result?
- What does this mean?
- How could you have done it differently?
- What benefits do you see? What detriments?
- What is your evidence?
- Why was it important?
- What would you conclude?
- Give an example.
- What if?
- How come?
- I wonder . . .

Teacher Reflection: A Fresh Approach

I use the list of different types of questions you gave me all the time. They have added so much to my questioning sequence in my lessons. I feel like I have gone from the same old points to a whole new fresh approach. The variety questions have helped me spark different ideas and conversations with my students.

—1st-grade teacher

Let's look at a discussion in a 6th-grade class where the teacher uses various types of questions in a lesson.

Questions in the Classroom: Using Different Types of Questions

TEACHER: We have been reading different biographies in class. Who can explain why we are reading this genre? (clarification question)

CANDICE: You want us to learn about the history of different people.

TEACHER: Why do you think that might be my goal? (clarification question)

CANDICE: To help us know the good things the people did to impact our lives now.

TEACHER: Why might I want you to know this? (consequence question)

CANDICE: We can see how they overcame hardships and fought for what they believed in that made them important in our history.

TEACHER: If what you are saying is my motivation, tell us what value there is in reading these books. (evaluation question/point of view)

AMID: Can I answer that?

TEACHER: Do you mind if he jumps in here? (change question/ knowledge)

CANDICE: Sure.

AMID: You want us to learn how to face difficult situations and to see that we have to push ourselves even if it is hard.

CANDICE: And sometimes that means taking risks. (elaboration question/analysis)

CANDICE: Not in a way that can hurt us but in ways that you stretch yourself. Many of the people we are reading about became heroes because they tried to achieve things that would help others.

AMID: It is like you said to us when we were doing the food drive: It is for the greater good. The people in our biographies did their work for the greater good.

SUMMARY

Figure 3.4 offers a guide to help you remember some of the different approaches described in this chapter and to assist you in deciding which is the best for your style of instruction. Remember that it takes time and effort to construct questioning techniques, time for the teachers and students to feel comfortable with a new approach, and time during the daily instruction itself if stimulating discussions are to take place. But the rewards are great as students deepen their thinking, develop new interests, expand their creativity, and learn to participate in a diverse exchange of ideas.

Figure 3.4. Different Techniques for Asking Questions

General Categories	Lowery	Bloom	Costa
Closed	Narrow Instructional	Knowledge	Clarifying
Open	Broad Instructional	Comprehension	Cuing
Literal	Non-Instructional	Application	Focus
Inferential		Analysis	Probing
Metacognitive		Synthesis	
		Evaluation	

Action Items

1. Consider the following quote and reflect on how it compares with your beliefs about the educational journey.

    Critical thinking encourages students to take into account more than just content, more than just their own experience, more than just the wisdom of the world and the experiences of others. Questions facilitate the intellectual process, leading students to integrate all three areas into a harmonious, and essentially individual, whole. Thus critical thinking is the student's journey through ideas, not the teacher's journey, and the student's destination, not the teacher's. (Christenbury & Kelly, 1983, p. 3)

2. In your next classroom discussion, keep track of the number of questions you ask. Take time to note which students answered the questions. Is there a difference between the number of boys and girls who answer the questions? Do you have a tendency to ask the brighter students more questions? Do you have a tendency to ask one or several students the most questions? Are there any students whom you seem to avoid asking questions?

CHAPTER FOUR

Wait Time

To be on a quest is nothing more or less than to become an asker of questions.

—Sam Keen

If you observe a number of elementary and secondary classrooms, you will readily notice, as I have, that the tone changes as the grade levels change. In the earlier grades, the tone is interactive and conversational, with teacher-to-student engagement. It quickly changes to an inquisitional tone and form of teacher-to-student interaction. As I have observed this change, I find it interesting that the goal for our older students is to support their development into mature, abstract thinkers who can think through problems and questions and respond with complex ideas and plans. Yet, as I observe upper-grade classes, most have an examination-type environment in which the responses do not involve higher-level thinking. The majority of middle and secondary classes have questions that are closed or recitational in nature. The goal of the Questioning Cycle is to change this, and the next step in the cycle, which is wait time, is critical in the process.

WHAT IS WAIT TIME?

Mary Budd Rowe (1978) is well known for her seminal work on wait time. Her experiments began as she listened to hundreds of recorded lessons. She found that "teachers asked between three and five questions per minute" with the results being that students could be involved with answering or hearing answered hundreds of questions in a day. The average wait time between the question and the answer was less than 1 second. In a few instances, the teacher used a longer pause or wait time. As Rowe listened to the recordings, she noticed that longer wait times created a change in the responses of the students. The inquisitional classroom, in which students and teachers "sometimes turned into adversaries—the inquisitor versus the prisoners on the dock," shifted and became a more thoughtful environment (p. 272). Dr. Rowe, therefore, decided to engage teachers in experiments where they agreed to wait 3 seconds or longer before students would respond to the question that was asked.

Other researchers have built on Rowe's research. They indicate that teachers have difficulty with wait time for many reasons, including the discomfort of silence, fear of embarrassing the students, and the stress of a packed curriculum (Walsh & Sattes, 2005, p. 18). Teachers need to understand that the goal of wait time is to produce highly effective responses that lead to genuine thinking and understanding. Although this may initially be uncomfortable, if a teacher waits for 3 to 5 seconds for a response, it gives the students time to formulate their thinking and to respond more appropriately to the question. At first, wait time may seem strange to the students. They are not used to the silence, and neither is the teacher. Therefore, when first using wait time, it is important for the teacher to explain the change and the purpose of wait time. Teachers can also start with 2 seconds the first week and then move to 3 seconds after that in order to help the shift to wait time occur more naturally.

To make wait time successful, teachers should understand that it takes students time to get used to the silence and to the idea that the teacher actually values their thinking. Teachers need to begin slowly with this component, and they should reassure students that they are really looking for the students' thoughts, not memorized facts. The teacher has to demonstrate that the students can trust the teacher's reaction to their thinking. This change gradually occurs as students are repeatedly engaged in this process, as they come to understand its purpose, and as they have sufficient time to explore the idea or controversy. They come to recognize that responses are about their real thoughts and ideas and that the teacher wants them to share as much information as they have on the concept that is being discussed.

Teachers will also use wait time after the student responds in order to formulate the follow-up question and to allow other students to think about the first student's response to the question. This means that there are actually two wait times involved with the question.

EFFECTS OF WAIT TIME

Students often may not have many adults in their lives who listen to them. Although it is hard to believe, Rowe's documentation shows that teachers often wait less than a second before they call on a student to answer a question. I have been in high school classes where there virtually is no wait time. Yet the research is clear: Students' responses improve when teachers allow for as little as 3 to 5 seconds of wait time. In effect, when students have the chance to stop, think, and reflect about what has been asked before they respond, they increase the length of their responses. In other research, it has been found that providing students with 3 to 5 seconds of wait time produced responses that were more confident and complex (Barnette, Orletski, Sattes, & Walsh, 1995; Fusco, 1983; Rowe, 1974, 1986). Moreover, this research also noted that teachers gave more skilled students more wait time than less skilled students (Tobin, 1987). These multiple sources support the need for teachers to monitor their use of wait time as a vehicle to build reflective or metacognitive processing in all the subjects that they teach (Atwood & Wilen, 1991). For teachers, this means that when students are given time to use their metacognitive (ability to reflect on one's own thinking) skills before they respond, they are more apt to consider their response in relationship to the question asked.

Overall, the experiments using wait time show that it has the following beneficial effects on students' and teachers' behaviors:

1. The length of students' responses increases.
2. The number of unsolicited but appropriate responses by students increases.
3. Failure to respond decreases.
4. The incidence of speculative thinking increases.
5. Teacher-centered show-and-tell decreases and child-child comparing increases.
6. The number of questions asked by children increases and the number of experiments they propose increases.
7. Contributions by "slow" students increase.
8. Disciplinary moves decrease.
9. Teachers' responses exhibit greater flexibility.
10. The number and kind of questions by the teacher change.
11. Teachers' expectations for the performance of certain children seem to change. (Rowe, 1978, pp. 281–285; Walsh & Sattes, 2005, pp. 8–86)

WAIT TIME IN THE QUESTIONING CYCLE

After taking the time to prepare and ask the question, the teacher now takes the third step in the Questioning Cycle and gives students the time they need to think about their ideas and formulate their answers. Whether the question is literal or inferential, the teacher needs to wait for students to think and mull over their ideas before they respond. When a teacher stops and uses wait time, it gives the youngster time to respond to the question, and the learner receives a clear message: "I value your opinion and respect the fact that you are thinking."

Teacher Reflection: Wait Time

I feel that I am improving in my questioning skills and the use of wait time. I used to think that I used wait time, but now I count in my head as you suggested. I notice that the responses are much better as compared to when they don't have enough wait time. I also noticed that in the past, I would talk during the wait time and say, "Let's see some different hands." Now I stay silent, which is sometimes hard. When I am silent, things happen. Last week I taught a lesson on helping verbs and a boy named Willy raised his hand. . . . He almost never raises his hand. He gave a well-thought-out answer. I was so proud of both of us.

—3rd-grade teacher

Teachers often short-circuit the process and do not allow for wait time. The reasons for this vary. Initially, students may not be comfortable with wait time. They may not believe that a teacher really wants them to think through the question and their response. They may believe that a teacher simply wants them to restate what has been taught or to respond with some answer the teacher already knows. Students often believe that answering a question is a guessing game and that their answers have to mirror what the teacher is thinking. Teachers, for these reasons and others, give up using wait time. But when they give this strategy time to become part of the dynamics of instruction, change happens.

STRATEGIES FOR WAIT TIME

There are some strategies a teacher can use to help students with wait time. Recently, I visited a 2nd-grade class where the teacher had one student act as timekeeper; this was the student's job for the day. The room was silent after a question, and only when the timekeeper gave the signal could the students raise their hands. This strategy creatively reinforced the idea of wait time with the students. But for me, it was a little too rigid. So I asked the youngsters their opinion of having a timekeeper. Nicole, a shy-looking dark-eyed girl, responded: "Mrs. T wanted to stop having a timekeeper. But we like it. I like it a lot. I know that I have time to think about the question. I used to give up quickly but now I think more. I have more time."

Teachers can build metacognitive strategies that are beneficial to encouraging students' thinking during wait time. This process requires that the teacher explains to students that "you need to think and understand how your idea fits into what the group is discussing at this time." The teacher can model a series of questions that students can ask themselves as they think about the question (Fountain & Fusco, 1991). These metacognitive questions include:

- What is my thinking on this question?
- Why do I think this?
- How does this fit into what we are learning?

Teachers who involve students in thinking about their responses have interesting results. In one 6th-grade classroom, I worked with a teacher who decided to modify my metacognitive questions. He found that he needed to support his students with this idea of wait time, and they agreed. To help with this, they created and posted the following rules for their class when questions are asked:

- I will carefully listen to the question.
- I will think of how to respond to the question.
- I will think about why this is a good answer.
- I will think of evidence to support my answer.
- I will compare my answer with the answers of my classmates who were called on to answer the question.

Questions in the Classroom:
An Illustration of Wait Time in the Questioning Cycle

The following discussion occurred in an 8th-grade class where the students were used to using the questioning cycle, wait time, and follow-up questions.

> TEACHER: We have been discussing the election and the changes that may occur as a result of it. Let's take a look back in time and see what we remember about the voting process. Who can tell me the year when women were given the right to vote? (Teacher pauses 6 seconds.) I notice no hands are up. Anyone want to take a guess? (Teacher waits 4 seconds.) Now we have a few hands. I will let you think another few seconds. (Teacher pauses again.) Nicholas, what do you think?

NICHOLAS: Before or during the Civil War.

TEACHER: (Waits 4 seconds.) Why do you think that?

NICHOLAS: (Hesitates.) I'm not sure, but I think it happened then because Lincoln wanted to free the slaves, and so he probably gave everyone the right to vote at the same time.

ANDREA: (Jumps in.) Are you saying women were slaves until that time?

TEACHER: Think for a moment, Andrea, is that what he said? (Waits 4 seconds.) Let's give Nicholas a chance to explain what he was saying.

NICHOLAS: (Directs his comment to Andrea.) I didn't say they were slaves, but they might as well have been, since they really didn't have rights like the men did and they had to work hard. Isn't that true? They were not equal citizens.

RAFE: (Jumps in and speaks to Nicholas.) Presidents just don't give you rights. A law had to be passed for women to vote. Right?

TEACHER: (Waits 4 seconds.) Let's hold on to those two points for a few minutes. I want to add a few more questions. What was the attitude of men toward women during the Civil War? (A few hands go up, and the teacher waits 5 seconds.)

CAROLE: Women were not seen as capable as men. They were capable to take care of the children and home or farm, but not much more.

TEACHER: (Waits 4 seconds.) Are women more capable today than they were earlier in our society? (Pauses 3 seconds.)

CAROLE: No, they probably actually worked harder because they didn't have all that we have today, like electricity. They really had to work hard to feed their families and take care of their homes and farms.

TEACHER: You see women as working harder.

ANDREA: (Jumping in.) Yeah! They had to do a lot for their families, so eventually the men decided to let them vote.

TEACHER: (Pauses 4 seconds.) I am a little confused. Am I hearing they got to vote because they were working hard during the Civil War? That's how they got to vote?

ANITA: No, they passed an amendment.

TEACHER: Which amendment, and when did that happen?

ANITA: (3-second pause.) I think it was the 21st Amendment, and women fought for it. I am not sure which one it was, but I know that there were women who fought to get the right to vote.

TEACHER: (Pauses 2 seconds.) How do you know that?

ANITA: I saw a statue in Washington, D.C., about one woman, and we read some books about women when we were in elementary school, but I don't remember their names.

TEACHER: Well, we have some ideas and questions and memories. It seems we need to do some reviewing and check out what we have discussed and see how accurate we have been. Anita, will you check and see which amendment gave women the right to vote and in which year? Nicholas, would you check the Civil War and see if women could vote during that time? Does anyone remember the name of any women who were involved with women getting the right to vote? (Pauses 6 seconds.)

MARGARITA: There was a Stanton woman. I remember her name because my grandmother has the same name.

TEACHER: Any others?

CHANDRA: How about Susan B. Anthony? Wasn't she involved?

TEACHER: All right, Chandra and Margarita, would you check and see what you can find out about these women? While they are checking, I am going to read an article about Esther Morris. I would like you to listen and take notes and see how she fits into our discussion about women's rights and elections. Then we will see what the others have turned up.

In an interview I had with the teacher after this lesson, he indicated that he was surprised at what his students did not know or recall. It changed the direction for his teaching because he recognized from the discussion that the students really did not know very much.

USING WAIT TIME FOR DIFFERENTIATED INSTRUCTION

As teachers become more conscious of each individual student's needs, involvement, and abilities, their self-regulation and self-awareness help them diagnose students' strengths and weaknesses. This will have an effect on how teachers use wait time. When I was teaching a 6th-grade group a unit on tolerance, I selected the poem "Perhaps" by Randy Guilhas. The questions I devised were aimed at the different ability levels of my students, and are shown, along with the poem, in Figure 4.1.

I was surprised by a comment that one student, Joseph, made during the discussion on discrimination that followed:

Discrimination is not only about color, it is about all kinds of things. If you are not smart or athletic, you experience discrimination. So the poet's words, "leaving dignities intact," were important to me because I get teased a lot and feel discriminated against when we play games at recess.

Figure 4.1. Bloom Question for the Poem "Perhaps"

"Perhaps" by Randy Guilhas

Perhaps if we were blinded
to the color of our skin
and we could view the essence
of intentions from within

Perhaps in revelation
from perception of repose
the you and me and us and we
become portions of the whole

Perhaps if we were deafened
to the language of the tongue
the mind then unconditioned
by believings we've become

Perhaps we'd witness wisdom
speak from new enlightened wealth
what one brings upon another
is then brought upon the self

Perhaps without the cravings
of the feeble flesh we wear
we then could be enlightened
in the spirit that we share

If we keep an oath of honor
leaving dignities intact
and render only kindness
we could change the world perhaps

© Copyright rguilhs 2006

Knowledge:
Why is the poem called "Perhaps"?
Tell what the poet means by the first stanza.
What does the word "dignity" mean in this poem?

Comprehension:
Give a summary of the poem.
What is the author saying we could perhaps change?
Select a line in the poem where the author presents a hopeful tone.

Application:
What factors change if we look past someone's physical characteristics?
Compare an instance in this poem to something you have witnessed.
What would change in our societies if we rendered kindness?
What would you add to this poem?

Analysis:
How would the world change if we kept an oath of honor leaving dignities
    intact?
What is the underlying theme of this poem?
Identify the techniques the poet describes that will help end discrimination.

Synthesis:
What would be your proposal that would change the world?
What are the poet's motives for writing this poem?
How would you change this poem to make it more powerful?

Evaluation:
How would you assess the effectiveness of the poet's words in ending
    discrimination?
Which stanza do you think best reflects what we can do to change the world?
    Why?
Tell your opinion of the title "Perhaps." Was it a good choice? Why?

The room had a heavy silence, and I allowed 6 seconds of wait time—even more than usual. When students began to respond there was a sense of embarrassment, but a beginning awareness of the different types of discrimination began to emerge.

Wait time is particularly important for students who may struggle in traditional classrooms. It is a gesture of respect from the teacher, and students come to realize that they are allowed to think before they respond. Wait time forces impulsive youngsters to pause, think, and elaborate on their responses, and it encourages all students to think and justify their answers and to reflect and be more systematic in their thoughts. The discussion time also helps introverted students because questions are asked more than one time, so shy children have time to think through a response during the discussion. Finally, wait time gives ELL students (English Language Learners) time to deal with the language barrier and compose their responses. We will add to the impact of differentiated instruction and the Questioning Cycle in later chapters.

BUILDING AWARENESS

As this chapter has shown, wait time in the Questioning Cycle helps teachers involve students and discover what they are thinking. Students can sense when the teacher is interested in their response and when the teacher is merely fishing for a specific answer. If the teacher allows ample wait time and shows respect for students' thoughtful contributions, the class gradually becomes aware that this is a genuine discussion, that everyone can and should respond, and that everyone's ideas are important. Often, like the teacher, students are surprised by the direction the discussion takes. I did not expect Joseph to make the comment about his feelings on discrimination, but it led some students to broaden their perspective of the concept of tolerance and to realize that discrimination has many faces.

For me, this is the heart of the matter. Because the Questioning Cycle follows a natural path of conversation and all students can respond, ideas and feelings emerge that would not ordinarily be heard in a standard classroom lecture environment. Thus, students of all ability levels feel the power of their contributions.

Action Items

1. Write about your experience with wait time. Then meet with a colleague and discuss and compare your reactions to wait time.
2. In reflecting on your classroom instruction, what difficulties do you have with wait time?
3. Visit another classroom and watch the teacher's interactions with the students. Does the teacher use wait time, and what do you notice about the results?

CHAPTER FIVE

Effective Listening

Careful listening is critical if students are to gain maximum benefit from lessons. This type of listening communicates to the students that the teacher has respect and values their ideas.

—Carolyn Hughes

Rewarding though it may be, the Questioning Cycle takes work. First, the teacher has to organize the unit, establish a focus with essential questions, plan lessons to guide the discussion, and then engage the students with questions. But once this happens, there is no time to relax. Once the teacher has asked the questions, the teacher must shift into the role of an active listener. The teacher's job is to use the wait time to guide and assess the direction of the discussion so that knowledge continues to be built around the concepts and guiding questions of the lesson.

In the following example, a 4th-grade class is involved with an author study of Chris Van Allsburg. The students know something about his style of writing, and they know to look for clues to the author's real meaning and intent. They have just finished reading *The Stranger*. Jacqueline, their teacher, begins her audiotaped lesson with an inferential question. The objective of the lesson is to have students look for clues to determine who "the stranger" is in the story.

Questions in the Classroom: The Stranger

TEACHER: As we were reading the story, I asked you to look for clues about the stranger. Who is the stranger? (Waits 4 seconds and then listens to responses.) Louisa, tell me what you are thinking.

LOUISA: He is a man that is responsible for the foliage. (Pauses 3 seconds.)

TEACHER: I am not sure what you mean that he is responsible for the foliage. Explain how you came to think that. (Pause. Teacher asks for elaboration and analysis.)

LOUISA: Well, without him the leaves don't change their color as they usually have done in the fall. (Pauses 3 seconds.)

TEACHER: What evidence do you have for your conclusion? (Pauses 4 seconds.)

LOUISA: The leaves stopped changing colors while the stranger stayed with the Baileys. Remember, in the story it said that to the south the leaves were green, and to the north they had changed their colors. The color changing stopped at the Bailey farm. (Pauses 2 seconds.)

TEACHER: Why do you think they did not change their colors, if he was responsible for the foliage? (Pauses 4 seconds.)

LOUISA: He wasn't doing his duty because he had the accident. (Pauses 2 seconds.)

TEACHER: What do you mean by "his duty?" (Pauses 4 seconds.)

LOUISA: His job was to go around and change the colors of the leaves. After he got hit by the car, he forgot that he should be doing this. Remember how he looked at the trees when he was on the hill? (Pauses 5 seconds.)

TEACHER: I remember that he did do that. Who is the stranger? (Pauses 3 seconds. Repeats the question.)

ARJUN: (Jumping in.) Do you want a name for him? (Pauses 4 seconds.)

TEACHER: Do you think I am looking for his name?

ARJUN: I agree with Louisa and I think he is either fall or father nature. (Pauses 3 seconds.) And your next question is going to be why I think that, right? (Teacher laughs. Pauses 2 seconds.) It's because nature changes the leaves and he is a man, so he has to be father nature, not mother nature. (Pauses 4 seconds.)

QUINN: (Jumps in.) Or, maybe he is Jack Frost.

TEACHER: Quinn, can you elaborate on your thinking?

QUINN: Louisa said he changed the colors of the leaves. Well, mother nature makes things come alive, like in springtime. Jack Frost kills the plants and leaves. The stranger is a man, so maybe Van Allsburg must want us to think he is Jack Frost, because he is a man changing the tree colors.

THOMAS: Jack Frost, that's a pretty cool idea. He was writing about nature and he gets us to think about the nature of both a man and a woman.

In the discussion, note how the teacher respectfully listened to the ideas of her students. She responded to their answers with follow-up questions. She used wait time and then listened attentively, asking the students to think more about their ideas. Her students also listened patiently and respectfully to one another and then used the information they gathered from one another to continue the discussion. Jacqueline asked her students to provide evidence for their answers and allowed other students to jump into the discussion. Students built on the responses and came up with a variety of ideas.

Students must have this type of experience with answering questions and must know that their responses will be listened to respectfully. Also, students should have the opportunity to learn that they can change their minds based on a discussion, or that they can agree to disagree. These exchanges are, or should be, part of a realistic discussion. Students will come to recognize that discussions can impact their knowledge and influence their thinking. Wen Ma (2006) further elaborates on this idea. He writes that these discussions are useful to students because they build language skills and develop

> critical thinking skills and interpretational strategies for learning. In these dialogues students can intellectually wrestle and grapple with viable voices of other fellow students and the teacher, dialogues with voices embedded in a text, and dialogue with overt and covert voices. (p. 33)

The impact of such discussions is that students' thinking shifts and they begin to learn to analyze what they hear. This skill is important in the classroom and in the world that we live in today.

What I find as a teacher and an observer is that students observe the teacher and then imitate the teacher's behavior. Jacqueline demonstrated that she is a good listener who values and analyzes what her 4th-grade students are saying. Her interpretations lead to her follow-up questions, which show her students the importance of their participation. Students begin to realize the value of good listening from this daily occurrence in their classroom.

This concept of good listening is elaborated on in the book *Listening: It Can Change Your Life* (Steil, Summerfield, & DeMare, 1983).The authors state that the benefits of listening include:

> The ability to establish relationships by listening attentively, to reduce tensions by empathetic listening, to solve problems and help others solve them by listening carefully, to stimulate others to do their best by attentiveness, to draw out the experiences of others, to take the fullest advantage of the knowledge and experience of those who wish to inform you to teach you, to increase cooperation and win friends, and to speed the development of ideas and projects. In addition to all of these personal benefits, the world is opened up to those who listen. (p. 123)

LISTENING

In effective classroom instruction, our goal is to produce students who can use listening strategies to build their vocabulary and language skills and improve their listening comprehension. An underpinning of reading comprehension is listening comprehension. Through the Questioning Cycle, students learn to participate in conversations and to analyze the quality of the discussion in order to make informed contributions to the discussion. This adds to their ability to put information together so that they can better comprehend it. They learn that listening is an active process that involves rephrasing ideas. As the teacher listens to students, he or she models the type of listening behavior expected of students and required by most state standards. Students are expected to listen with a purpose and to

- Be respectful
- Stay focused on the speaker and not be preoccupied with what they want to say next
- Avoid interruptions
- Take the speaker's comments seriously
- Gather information and understand the facts
- Be open-minded and refrain from judgments
- Analyze and interpret the information being stated
- Use the information they need to know from the speaker to add, clarify, extend, or formulate their own knowledge
- Build on the concept that is being discussed

The Questioning Cycle provides the opportunity for these behaviors through the different types of questions and responses that are given. Students and teachers who use the Questioning Cycle come to understand that active listening is important in order to gain further knowledge.

As you read the dialogue regarding *The Stranger*, did you notice how the students built on the responses, how they responded to the questions that the teacher asked, and how they were comfortable with her continually following up with more questions? One student even anticipated the teacher's follow-up question. Clearly, students in this class were used to this type of interaction.

In the dialogue, the teacher carefully listened to the students' responses and did not interrupt. This model is sometimes difficult for teachers to initiate because they are:

- Used to helping students respond and to finishing their answers;
- Fearful that the response is going to be incorrect and don't want the child to be embarrassed;
- Concerned that the response is incorrect and want to make sure the class gets the right information; and
- Insecure about the process of questioning.

Listening is a complicated process that varies from situation to situation. From an early age, students sense when it is important to listen and when they can tune the speaker out. They also become convinced that they can learn from certain people and not from others. When teachers listen to the complete responses of their students, they foster an atmosphere of respect. Over time, this atmosphere allows even insecure students to venture forth and respond. They begin to recognize that their ideas and opinions are really of interest to the teacher and their peers. When students see the teacher listening, they often recognize that they, too, should be listening because there may be something that they can learn, understand, or contribute to in the discussion. Thus, the Questioning Cycle with its use of wait time becomes an opportunity to develop better classroom listeners.

Teachers also have an opportunity to build students' responses by reminding them of the different ways they can be listening. For example, students learn that they can listen to, gather, and analyze information, or that they can hear how an idea is being interpreted (Roe & Ross, 2006). Guiding students to understand what kind of listening and thinking occurs when different types of questions are asked supports students in their participation. They learn that effective listening involves interpreting the information and determining when and if they should respond. Just this process alone is important to learn because it teaches students how to function in a conversation.

When I was doing a literature research study, I found this to be true with 6th-, 7th-, and 8th-grade students (Fusco, 1983).The more I listened to them and followed up with questions, the more information students shared with me. Once they trusted that I would really listen, they were comfortable showing me their knowledge. Tobin (1987) found that if teachers carefully listen and wait when the students respond, and if the teachers do not immediately speak, students often will go ahead and provide additional information in their responses. What seems to happen is that students let down their guard when they think the teacher is really interested in the contributions that they are making.

QUESTIONS

It is thus important for teachers to recognize that effective listening is a fundamental that must be taught and well understood because it has a profound impact on learning (Thompson, Leintz, Nevers, & Witkowski, 2004). Along with this, what begins to happen is that students once again find their voices and begin to ask further questions related to what is being taught.

The following questions demonstrate the type of questions students ask when careful listening has provoked them to think:

- Frederick Douglass believed in freedom. But not everyone else did. Why is that? (2nd-grade boy)
- Symbolism is hard to put into your writing. How long does it take a writer to learn how to do this? Will I ever be able to really do it this year? (5th-grade girl)
- Why do people write so much about teenagers? Do they really understand what it is like to feel the way we do? Would it be better to have teenage authors? (7th-grade girl)
- Why do so many men in Congress get into trouble? How can we trust them to make our laws when they break so many? (8th-grade boy)

Let's return to the dialogue in Jacqueline's 4th-grade class about *The Stranger*.

LORI: (Jumps in.) Thomas, are you saying that Van Allsburg is saying that men like to kill things?

MARISA: (Jumps in.) My father loves to plant in the garden. He doesn't kill things, and he gets upset when things die.

TEACHER: Thomas, can you clarify your thinking for Lori and Marisa?

THOMAS: I think Van Allsburg was taking facts that we know and putting them into his story. We all know Jack Frost brings fall and cold weather. The plants die and the leaves change their colors. The main character in *The Stranger* is a man. So Van Allsburg could not call him mother nature because it wouldn't fit.

LISA: But mother nature does let things die . . . flowers only last for a while. He used Jack Frost because we know he changes the leaves and that is why there was frost on the window, too. That was one of his clues.

NICHOLAS: (Jumps in.) Then is this story about a comparison of the people in nature, or is the story about how things change, or is it about weather and the seasons?

TEACHER: That's an interesting question. What do you think?

The discussion continues as the students not only establish the identity of the stranger but go on to discuss the main ideas of the story.

Jacqueline's classroom discussion not only demonstrates her ability to listen and follow up with questions but also shows that her students have learned these skills. In the next chapter, we will explore the thinking of teachers like Jacqueline in order to understand how they design their follow-up questions.

Action Items

1. What is your attitude about listening? Are you a good listener? How can you assess your own listening skills?
2. List the strategies that you use to build listening skills in your students. Meet with a colleague or mentor and discuss your list. See whether their list has additional strategies you can add to your list.

CHAPTER SIX

Assessing Responses and Preparing Follow-Up Questions

Units and assessments are always works in progress that come alive only when they are mediated by students' interests, backgrounds and questions.

—Giselle Martin-Kniep

Previous chapters discussed the assessment that teachers do early in the Questioning Cycle. In planning your questions, you assess students' backgrounds, their prior experience with the concepts, their interest in the topic, and their relevant skill levels. Let's now examine how students' responses to your questions can support classroom assessment.

The general purpose of assessment is to create more effective instruction (Lowery, 1989), but how does a teacher discover what students are thinking and learning? Teachers have two avenues that provide valuable assessment information. The first occurs through students' written responses; the second is through their verbal responses. Although written responses are undeniably important, teachers must be cautious in using writing as an assessment tool. In many classrooms, there are students who possess a range of writing processing problems. Several students may be poor spellers or have handwriting problems, and these students' writing difficulties—an inability to express the scope and depth of their understanding—may mask their actual conceptual knowledge. Oral responses provide these students, in particular, with another opportunity to demonstrate what they know. Even if some students also have difficulty with oral presentations, in a classroom where discussions and conversation are frequent and encouraging, oral skills flourish because students are more willing to share their knowledge with the teacher and their peers.

In assessing responses, sometimes the teacher discovers that the students already know the concept or skill being taught, and sometimes he or she realizes that the students are a long way from understanding.

> ### Teacher Reflection: Assessing Responses
>
> I feel that questioning is the main channel to really find out if the children are understanding what you are teaching as well as having them retain the information. Although I try to be conscious of my questioning, I realize that I tend to keep my questions very basic and simple. I think I partly do this because I am not sure the children are capable of answering some of my questions and I also want a correct answer. Learning about assessing the responses has helped me a lot even though it makes more work in my head. I listen more now to what the kid is saying and think about it so I ask a better question back. This is hard because I still want the right answers. I think it is going to take a long time for me to give this up. I try to keep in mind that this is about the kids' thinking and not about me. I think it is a "new teacher" problem.
>
> —4th-grade teacher

Appraising the inadequate or misleading evidence of students' understanding is part of the structuring of the learning process (McTighe & Wiggins, 1999). This ongoing assessment helps teachers to make informed decisions about subsequent instruction, and to recognize when to expand the level of the concept sooner rather than staying at the lowest level of comprehension. This is a critical part of teaching: understanding when to spiral the concept upward and when to re-teach the concept and think through what is really necessary to build understanding.

ASSESSING STUDENT RESPONSES: THE SOLO METHOD

When listening to students, teachers must consider the level of complexity in their responses. How much information has the student actually provided? What does the student's answer really say about what has been comprehended?

One method of assessment is the SOLO Taxonomy (Structure of the Observed Learning Outcomes) by Biggs and Collis (1982). Their approach provides a very practical, five-level structure to assess student understanding:

- *Prestructural:* The student does not provide any information in the answer that demonstrates an understanding of the concept.

- *Unistructural:* The student's response provides a simple understanding or detail.
- *Multistructural:* The student's response provides many facts that are not part of a main idea and do not go beyond the literal level of understanding.
- *Relational:* The student shows an understanding in which facts and main ideas are integrated. There is an understanding beyond what has been read or discussed.
- *Extended Abstract:* The student's response is more sophisticated and demonstrates an integration of concepts at an abstract level. (pp. 24–27)

To better understand the application of this taxonomy, let's take a simple question that a 5th-grade teacher asked. A group of students were reading *Night Journey* (Avi, 1979). The teacher began by asking the question, "Who is Peter?" Below are the actual answers provided by students who were in the same group and supposedly had similar reading abilities. Their understanding and responses showed a great deal of variation, however. Each level is illustrated by a different student's response.

- *Prestructural:* Peter is a boy.
- *Unistructural:* Peter is a boy that goes to live with Mr. Shinn.
- *Multistructural:* Peter's parents die and he has to go to live with Mr. Shinn who is a Quaker. He doesn't liking sharing his horse with Mr. Shinn. He is not happy living with him. He discovers and helps the runaway indentured servants.
- *Relational:* Peter is the main character in the book and he is a hero because he helps and protects the children.
- *Extended Abstract:* Peter is a hero because he helps the children get away. He is not like Mr. Shinn. He knows that laws are made to protect people and should be followed. But when laws hurt people then they should be broken to help the people, especially if they are in danger.

This sequence of responses illustrates several points.

1. If teachers take time to listen to several students' responses, they can get divergent responses to the same question.
2. In a supportive environment, students will build on one another's responses.
3. When students build on one another's responses, they can extend literal questions by analyzing and synthesizing, thus creating inferential responses.

The SOLO Taxonomy thus helps teachers to assess the level of students' responses and enables them to construct an appropriate follow-up question that will encourage students to elaborate on their thinking, apply their knowledge to new situations, or discover alternatives to their own ideas.

PREPARING FOLLOW-UP QUESTIONS

After assessing students' responses, the immediate next step in the Questioning Cycle is to ask appropriate follow-up questions. This is a crucial step. It is well established that students need the feedback that proper follow-up provides. For example, a meta-analysis of eight studies indicated that students who received relevant feedback performed significantly better on achievement measures than students who did not receive the feedback (Marzano, Pickering, & Pollock, 2001).

In thinking about follow-up questions, teachers should consider:

The Question	The Response	Follow-up Question
What concept is being developed by the question?	What is the level of the response?	What part of the response do I want to explore with the student?

Educator Carolyn Hughes presented a workshop in 1987 in which she provided a list of follow-up question types. Although not exhaustive, her list is a valuable resource. It can be found in the book *Quality Questioning* (Walsh & Sattes, 2005). Let's look at Hughes's list and apply it to a series of questions that I observed in a lesson on letter writing (Hughes, 1987/1988).

- *Variety:* Variety questions are used when more or different responses are wanted. This type of follow-up question is also helpful when only one area of a broad topic has been noted by the students. EXAMPLE: What are some different reasons people might have for writing a letter?
- *Clarification:* A clarification question is used to help pupils clarify a word meaning or idea. This type of question is based on the recognition that some pupils may not understand the same words or may have different definitions of a given term. EXAMPLE: What are you thinking of when you say this is the body of the letter?
- *Refocus:* Refocusing is indicated if the pupil is bringing in extraneous matter or is off-focus in using a thinking skill such

as recall when a difference is needed. EXAMPLE: You are telling us about a letter of the alphabet. Now tell us what you observed about this letter.

- *Narrow Focus*: When the broad starter questions do not bring out specific essential ideas, narrow focus questions are needed. EXAMPLE: In a letter, what does the greeting tell you?
- *Specification*: This type of follow-up question is used when the response is general. EXAMPLE: Yes, the letter has different parts, and I would like you to tell me exactly what they are.
- *Extension*: The situation calling for extension is the reverse of that for specification. Extension questions follow responses that are fragmented or incomplete. EXAMPLE: You told us there is a name at the bottom. How is that different from the name at the top?
- *Verification*: Accuracy of information is ascertained by use of verification to explain the reasoning used or to help the pupil check inaccurate data. EXAMPLE: How do you know that Roger is the sender of the letter?
- *Support*: When a classification has been made or an inference given, a support question is usually needed to guide the student to give the basis for the label or inference. EXAMPLE: How did you decide those words are metaphors?

These questions help demonstrate how the follow-up question can be used to extend students' thinking and expand their ability to further analyze their understanding of a concept that is being taught. Figure 6.1 provides a graphic overview of the process.

Figure 6.1. Objectives of Lessons in Content and Guiding Questions

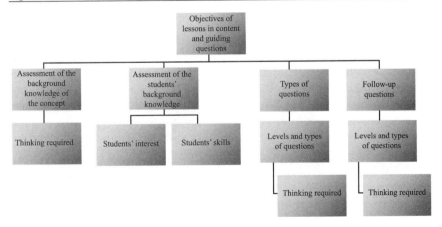

In the following discussion, notice how the follow-up questions stimulate these 4th-grade students to reply in a way that reveals a deeper level of understanding.

Questions in the Classroom: Extending Responses

TEACHER: Let's re-read this page: "I want to be beautiful but not so beautiful that a train moving in the sun like a metal peacock's glowing feather on tracks that are like stilts a thousand miles long laid down like a ladder up a flat mountain (wow!) seems dull." (Moss, 1993, p. 15

TEACHER: What kind of connection do you think of as you read this passage? (specification)

JACOB: I have good feelings inside. (unistructural)

TEACHER: What do you mean? (clarification)

JACOB: I see a beautiful peacock with lots of colors shining and I like the feeling I get from seeing beautiful things. (multistructural)

TEACHER: For you, this passage creates a beautiful image. What else can someone add to this discussion? (variety)

SARAH: Well, it is a simile, too. (relational)

TEACHER: Tell us more about that idea. (extension)

SARAH: Well, the author has the girl comparing herself to things and the girl uses the word *like*. (multistructural)

TEACHER: Does that make it a simile? (support)

SARAH: I never thought that about train tracks being a ladder like stilts. So that is a simile. And the train is a metal peacock so that is a comparison because it really isn't. She does not really mean that the train is a peacock, she is creating the image and that is what a simile does. It compares things. (relational)

In this context, the teacher is not necessarily looking for a "correct" answer but instead is using questions to build cumulative learning or to encourage elaboration of an idea. No longer is a single answer a correct response to a question. Instead, all responses become valuable data and are appropriate because they reflect the students' cognitive levels. Responses are perceived as more than a mere retelling of the details of a text and become a vehicle for informal assessment of students' cognitive level and a guide for selecting appropriate future lessons.

Obviously, students' responses will comprise diverse answers that range from restatements to generalizations to hypotheses, and this range itself depends upon the concept contained in the lesson and the level of questions asked. Teachers might realize that more in-depth study is needed, that another avenue needs to be pursued, or that the student lacks interest in the topic. At its best, however, teacher-student interaction will reveal the depth of the students' understanding, as shown in the simile example above.

ANALYZING RESPONSES IN CONTEXT

Sometimes a student's unexpected response does not seem to match the question. In the following example from a kindergarten class, notice how the teacher redirects the student's focus by asking another question aimed at getting clarification of the student's thinking.

Questions in the Classroom: Letters

TEACHER: We have been talking about letters. Tell us, what is a letter? (variety)
SHARON: You can climb in a tree and get a cat.
TEACHER: What do you mean? (clarification)
SHARON: It means you climb.
TEACHER: What is my question? (refocus)
SHARON: What is a ladder?

Incorrect responses within the Questioning Cycle help teachers adjust their instruction. In the above case, the child responded to the question as he understood it. When a student does not respond to a question in an expected way, teachers can:

- provide more information to the students
- encourage students to rethink their ideas
- reconsider whether the question needs rewording
- refocus and have the student clarify and explain the response by providing evidence for his or her thinking

FROM INITIAL QUESTIONS TO FOLLOW-UP: A 6TH-GRADE BOOK DISCUSSION

Consider another example. In a 6th-grade class, the students have independently read the book *My Brother Sam Is Dead* by James Lincoln Collier

(Collier & Collier, 1974).A teacher has prepared a range of questions to use in a book discussion, including the essential question that will ultimately guide the discussion, and questions that aim to meet two state standard requirements.

Lesson's Essential Question: Why does Sam die?

Standard Key Ideas and Details:

1. Students will cite evidence to support analysis of what the text says explicitly as well as inferences drawn from the text.
2. Students will determine a central idea of a text and how it is conveyed through particular details.

The teacher prepares the following range of questions that will allow for the different abilities of the students in the group:

- What are the key characteristics of Sam and Tim? (knowledge, literal question)
- How are they alike? How are they different? (analysis, inferential question)
- What was Mr. Meeker's attitude toward the fighting between the colonists and the English soldiers? (knowledge, literal question)
- Why does Sam feel the colonists should fight the British? (analysis, inferential question)
- Describe Tim's attitude toward his brother Sam. (analysis, inferential question)
- Why does Sam join the army? (synthesis, inferential question)
- Why does Tim go to his brother's execution? (analysis, inferential question)
- Who really needed Brown Bess? Why? (evaluation, inferential question)
- Sam says, "That's Father for you . . . a chance on getting killed." What do you think are the principles Sam's talking about? (analysis, inferential question)
- What happens to Father? (comprehension, literal question)
- What does Sam mean when he says, "When I woke up I was different. I noticed it first at breakfast"? (synthesis, inferential question)
- If you were Sam, what would you have done? What if you were Tim? (evaluation, inferential and reflective question)
- Why does Sam die? (evaluation, inferential)

Aware that he or she can ask a knowledge question that will allow a number of students to respond, the teacher also recognizes the possibility that students may provide responses that range from the literal to the inferential. Let's look at the questions and the responses that were given by students from the audiotape made during the discussion.

Questions in the Classroom: Extending Responses

TEACHER: What was Mr. Meeker's attitude toward the fighting between the colonists and the English soldiers?

LIAM: He thought the English would win because they had the whole British army behind them and they had the king behind them. He thought it was just stupid . . . that they had no chance. (multistructural)

TEACHER: Does he actually say it is stupid, or are those your words? (verification)

LIAM: No, he says that. (unistructural)

KATIE: I thought it was more than that. I thought that he really didn't like Sam going off to war and stuff and that's why he was being so mean to Sam. I think he thought the British were going to win. (relational)

TEACHER: So, in a way, you are agreeing with Liam. Do you think he would have felt the same if he thought they were going to win? (clarification)

KATIE: I think he hated war. He was a Loyalist because he said no way are these guys are going to win this—no way. They had millions of people and we had hardly any people over here, and he thought there would be no good from men dying for no reason. He was afraid that his son was going to get killed fighting for a lost cause. He thought that there was no reason for war. He said it could be settled. I don't think it was about the war. I think he was afraid. (relational)

TEACHER: Afraid of what? (specification)

KATIE: His son getting killed. (unistructural)

TEACHER: What else can someone add to this? (extension)

TATIANA: The father didn't think a few taxes would do that much harm. Sam didn't really think that way. He wanted to fight for what he thought was right. But his father didn't agree with him. His father thought nothing would come out of this war, only men dying. (relational)

RICCO: I kind of agree with Tatiana. I think his father thought maybe Sam was really going to get killed. When Sam first left, he thought he'd be back in a few days but then after a few days he had the feeling that Sam wasn't going to be back even after the war. He wasn't coming back. He was going to be killed. (relational)

Because the students are actively engaged in the process and answering different types of questions, they ask their own questions in the discussion to clarify their understanding or confusion. Now, read another section from the same audiotape.

Questions in the Classroom: My Brother Sam Is Dead

TEACHER: Describe Tim's attitude toward his brother Sam. (specification)

TATIANA: He really likes his brother Sam, and one of his favorite things to do with Sam is when they would go to bed and Sam would just lay by his brother and keep him nice and warm, tell him stories . . . like how Sam charged up this hill and did things. He was so glorious, and Tim would want to be like Sam and wanted to show that he could do everything just as good as Sam . . . so Sam could be proud of him. (relational)

TEACHER: He really looked up to his brother. How does the father feel about this? (narrow focus)

LIAM: I think he is worried that he would follow him if he could. (multistructural)

JAIME: I got the impression that Tim really loved his brother and cared for him. At the end when they were going to kill him, he couldn't watch it when they shot him. I thought that was pretty sad when they did that right in front of him. I didn't understand why he even went and watched his brother die, given his feelings. (extended abstraction)

TEACHER: That's a good question. So, why does he go and see his brother get executed? (support)

As you read this section, the students' involvement is obvious. They ask questions and make connections and associations between ideas; they build their knowledge in a supportive environment that allows them to ask questions to clarify their perspective. The teacher's range and level of difficulty of questions invites students to participate at the different levels, and their responses allow for ongoing assessment of the knowledge being constructed.

ANOTHER EXAMPLE: A 1ST-GRADE DISCUSSION ABOUT FALL

Let's look at another interaction between a teacher and her 1st-grade students. They are conducting an exploration of what they know about fall. In the following two sections, we will explore what the teacher does. The first time allows you to read the whole exchange; the second section has comments in parentheses that illustrate what she was trying to accomplish. During the discussion, the teacher used an anecdotal record assessment form to keep track of the students' responses and participation. Her questions were designed to assess students' background knowledge of the concept of fall, and when and why things change. She expects that the students' answers will vary based on their different knowledge and that the answers may shift as students learn more about the concept. The teacher has selected questioning as a strategy because she believes that the students have enough background knowledge about fall and about the reasons for the changes that occur at this time of year. Note how the teacher stays with the students and uses follow-up questions.

Questions in the Classroom:
Assessing What Students Know About Fall

TEACHER: Let's look at the cover of the book. What do you think it might be about? Now, take your time and let's have some good thinking.

ELLEN: The fall.

TEACHER: What makes you think it is about the fall?

ELLEN: Because of the leaves.

TEACHER: Why do the leaves tell you it is fall?

ELLEN: Because they have colors in the fall.

TEACHER: Can they have colors any other time of the year?

ELLEN: No, only in the fall.

TEACHER: Please explain your answer a little more. Can they start changing colors in the summer?

ELLEN: No, it has to be the fall because then they fall off the trees.

TEACHER: Look out the window. Would you look around and see where there are leaves? Are there leaves on the ground?

ELLEN: Yes.

TEACHER: What colors do you see?

ELLEN: Some are green and some are brown.

TEACHER: If it isn't fall yet, how did that happen?

ELLEN: The rain made them fall, not fall.

TEACHER: The rain made them fall. What about the colors? Is there anything else you want to add to that about their colors?

ELLEN: No.

TEACHER: You have been thinking hard. Shall I give someone else a chance to do some more thinking? Would someone else like to add to this? What do you think the book might be about?

MARK: Hmmm . . . the leaves.

TEACHER: Leaves. What evidence do you have that the book is about leaves?

MARK: 'Cause I see them on the cover and squirrels, too. There will be leaves and squirrels in the story.

TEACHER: Why do you think I am going to read this book to you about leaves and squirrels?

MARK: 'Cause you like them.

TEACHER: Who can give us other reasons why I may be reading this book?

MARK: It's colorful.

TEACHER: So you think that I am reading this book because I like squirrels and leaves. Would anyone else like to predict what our story is going to be about and its connection to fall?

PAM: I think it is about the fall and leaves.

TEACHER: Why do you think that?

PAM: Because it's almost the fall.

TEACHER: Yes, fall starts Thursday, which is in 3 days. Ellen said that the leaves come down in the fall. Look out the window. Do we have leaves down outside right now like we see on the cover?

PAM: Yes.

TEACHER: So, can leaves change colors and fall even before it is fall?

PAM: No, it has to be fall. But . . . maybe they can.

TEACHER: Why do you say maybe they can?

PAM: I saw leaves fall and they were red and it wasn't raining. So, I think they can change even if it isn't fall.

TEACHER: Who else would like to add to our discussion before we start the book?

ROB: Why are there squirrels in the picture?

TEACHER: Why do you think?

ROB: It is fall.

TEACHER: Do we see squirrels in the spring and summer?

ROB: Yes.

TEACHER: Why do you think there are squirrels on the cover with the leaves?

Rob: Because they like to play in the leaves in the fall. I like to jump in them when my father rakes them.

Teacher: Jumping in leaves is fun in the fall. Let's see if anyone else wants to add to this before we read the book.

Dustin: Squirrels get acorns in the fall like Earl did in the other book we read.

Teacher: Do you remember why Earl and his mother were collecting the acorns?

Dustin: I think it is because they need food for winter.

Teacher: What do you think the book is about?

Dustin: About what happens in the fall and what squirrels do in the fall?

Teacher: I am going to read the book now. I want you to listen carefully so you can tell us what the book is about and how it connects to fall, leaves, and squirrels. See if you can discover any other reasons for the colored leaves being on the ground today even though it is not fall yet. When I am finished, I will ask you more questions about fall, leaves, and squirrels.

Now, let's review the teacher's actions and thinking during this discussion. (My comments are in parentheses for easier reading.) Remember that the types of questions serve as an advance organizer for the students by framing the potential ideas and purpose for what they may find in the story.

Teacher: Let's look at the cover of the book. What do you think it might be about? Now, take your time and let's have some good thinking.

Ellen: The fall.

Teacher: What makes you think it is about the fall?

Ellen: Because of the leaves.

Teacher: Why do the leaves tell you it is fall?

Ellen: Because they have colors in the fall.

Teacher: Can they have colors any other time of the year?

Ellen: No, only in the fall.

(The teacher is using a comprehension question at the literal level because the children can see the cover of the book. Then the teacher is following up the student's responses with questions to explore the child's thinking and to encourage the child to describe the concept of changing leaves and to be more specific. This is also designed to build the children's language skills. The question "Can they have colors any other time of the year?" changes the question to the application level as it explores the child's concept of change.)

> TEACHER: Please explain your answer a little more to me. Can they start changing colors in the summer?
> ELLEN: No, it has to be the fall because then they fall off the trees.
> TEACHER: Look out the window. Would you look around and see where there are leaves? Are there leaves on the ground?
> ELLEN: Yes.
> TEACHER: What colors do you see?
> ELLEN: Some are green and some are brown.
> TEACHER: If it isn't fall yet, how did that happen?
> ELLEN: The rain made them fall, not fall.
> TEACHER: The rain made them fall. What about the colors? Is there anything else you want to add to that about their colors?
> ELLEN: No.

(The teacher attempts to refocus the child and have her consider her faulty thinking. She gives clues to the discrepancy and asks a follow-up question about what might be the cause of change. The child does not recognize her faulty reasoning and maintains her perspective. Although she sees that the leaves have fallen down, her thinking is clouded by her concept that leaves fall and change colors only in the fall. She cannot reconcile the contradiction with the knowledge she has constructed in her head, and is unable to make a cognitive shift. The teacher is surprised by the response, makes an anecdotal notation of this, and makes a transition to the next student. The teacher moves on to get students to consider what the book is about.)

> TEACHER: You have been thinking hard. Shall I give someone else a chance to do some more thinking? Would someone else like to add to this? What do you think the book might be about?

(The teacher remains with the same question to continue to assess her students' knowledge and get a variety of responses about the concepts.)

> MARK: Hmmm . . . the leaves.
> TEACHER: Leaves. What evidence do you have that the book is about leaves?
> MARK: 'Cause I see them on the cover and squirrels, too. There will be leaves and squirrels in the story.

TEACHER: Why do you think I am going to read this book to you about leaves and squirrels?
MARK: 'Cause you like them.
TEACHER: Can you think of any other reasons why I may be reading this book?
MARK: It's colorful.

(Again, the teacher asks the same question, which is at the level of literal comprehension. The goal is to assess the student's understanding of fall, and Mark's response merely provides identification information, nothing about the cover of the book and its relationship to fall. Because his response provides no opportunity to add details to the discussion, the teacher moves on. The teacher records that Mark has not made the connection to the attributes of fall and needs more experience with the concept.)

TEACHER: So you think that I am reading this book because I like squirrels and leaves. Would anyone else like to predict what our story is going to be about and its connection to fall?

(The teacher redirects to the concept of fall, remaining with the literal comprehension question.)

PAM: I think it is about the fall and leaves.
TEACHER: Why do you think that?

(The teacher's response is designed to encourage Pam to elaborate on her thinking.)

PAM: Because it's almost the fall.
TEACHER: Yes, fall starts Thursday, which is in 3 days. Ellen said that the leaves come down in the fall. Let's look out the window. Do we have leaves down outside right now like we see on the cover?

(The teacher again tries to add to the concept and encourages the girl by asking her to compare the view outside with the book cover. This moves the thinking toward analysis, but it is important to create a comparison between the cover and the observed environment of the outdoors.)

PAM: Yes.
TEACHER: So, can leaves change colors and fall even before it is fall?
PAM: No, it has to be fall. But . . . maybe they can.

TEACHER: Why do you say maybe they can?

PAM: I saw leaves fall and they were red and it wasn't raining. So, I think they can change even if it isn't fall.

(The teacher is guiding the thinking and encouraging students to see the contradiction. The child sees the contradiction but is not quite sure of the concept. The teacher uses comparison questions to guide the thinking.)

TEACHER: Who else would like to add to our discussion before we start the book?

(Since the discussion is a back-and-forth exchange, Rob feels comfortable and jumps in with a question.)

ROB: Why are there squirrels in the picture?

TEACHER: Why do you think?

ROB: It is fall.

TEACHER: Do we see squirrels in the spring and summer?

ROB: Yes.

TEACHER: Why do you think there are squirrels on the cover with the leaves?

ROB: Because they like to play in the leaves in the fall. I like to jump in them when my father rakes them.

TEACHER: Jumping in leaves is fun in the fall. Let's see if anyone else wants to add to this before we read the book.

(The teacher's response to Rob's question is designed to get him to explain his thinking. This is a literal knowledge question. She then tries to engage him in a comparison question but he does not respond. The teacher notes and records that the Rob's comments are not adding to the discussion under way, nor to the knowledge she is attempting to scaffold. Notice that the teacher asked a follow-up question to clarify the response.)

DUSTIN: Squirrels get acorns in the fall like Earl did in the other book we read.

(The teacher notes that Dustin has made a text-to-text connection. He has connected information from one book to the book they are about to read. The teacher asks a follow-up question to clarify the response, hoping to build on the information regarding fall that was in the previously read book.)

TEACHER: Do you remember why Earl and his mother were collecting the acorns?

DUSTIN: I think it is because they need food for winter.

TEACHER: So, what do you think the book is about?

DUSTIN: About what happens in the fall and what squirrels do in the fall?

TEACHER: I am going to read the book now. I want you to listen carefully so you can tell me what the book is about and how it connects to fall, leaves, and squirrels. See if you can discover any other reasons for the colored leaves being on the ground today even though it is not fall yet. When I am finished, I will ask you more questions about fall, leaves, and squirrels. Remember, if you have any questions as I am reading, write them down on your question sheet.

(The teacher responds by asking a literal comprehension question designed to have the youngster do some interpretative thinking. Although Dustin has moved the conversation ahead, the teacher decides to leave the discussion here and use the book to build students' thinking. The teacher notes that the class does not appear to understand the concepts of fall and the change that takes place. This awareness will now drive her instruction.)

The teacher in this example was involved with the discussion and worked to make it more of a conversation. She engaged students and allowed them to clarify their ideas and verbalize their misconceptions. She learned, however, that her students did not understand the concept of fall. This classroom exchange conducted prior to the reading of the book consequently shifted her thinking about what she had believed the students understood, and thus broadened the scope of her future lessons. The teacher decided that her short- and long-term instructional goals (the reading of the book and related activities) would focus on the attributes of fall (that the days get cooler and shorter) and seek to enhance her students' ability to see the impact of fall on the environment. It was particularly interesting that the students readily used the word *fall* but that their concept of this content vocabulary word was not fully established. Although the students were not successful with the application question, the teacher still used it as a way to initiate inferential reasoning; she also hoped that the comparison between the book and the students' own environment would reshape their conceptual understanding. She hoped that the reading of the book would clarify why leaves fall and how animals prepare for winter.

The interactions in this example also display cognitive dissonance. The children's thinking is confused about fall, yet the children persever-ate with the notion that leaves fall only in autumn. They do not have the notion that the leaves fall because the weather is getting cooler. They do not understand what causes the change. They think that the leaves have to wait until the day fall arrives. Even though they can see the leaves on the ground, they are unable to change their perspective because they have not really discussed how climate affects the change. The teacher believes that reading the book will provide explanations, and that the children will have the opportunity to hear and then discuss the reality of how change takes place. They will note how the animals are beginning to prepare for the change as the weather begins to get cooler. What is important to note is that by using the Questioning Cycle, the teacher revised her appraisal of the students' knowledge of fall, and determined that she had to design lessons to address and remedy their current confusion and extend their concept of what causes the leaves to fall.

Supportive classroom discussions always make profound statements about respect. Although teachers can establish classroom rules to foster re-spect, behavior is always more telling. Even though the students were not clear about the concepts, the teacher continued to work at getting them to delve into their experiential background and to think hard about the con-cepts. The teacher responded to every child's answer, even when it was not really connected. In several cases, she attempted to get the children to ex-amine their thinking and to deal with the apparent discrepancies, and this was done in a respectful manner. In accepting the students' responses dur-ing the interaction, the teacher learned that the students did not fully com-prehend "fall" and the changes that it brings. Had she not gone through the process, she might have missed the fact that there was a gap between what she thought and what her students understood. Instead, she realized that her students were just beginning to organize their thoughts about fall and would need more experiences with the concepts. She knew that through asking and answering questions, her students were learning to:

- Clarify their ideas
- Listen and interact with others
- Reflect on what is being said
- Become responsible for participating
- Consider ideas
- Become risk-takers and share their ideas
- Become flexible in their thinking
- Build oral language skills
- Experiment with ideas

RE-PLANNING BASED ON STUDENTS' RESPONSE: "GRAND CONVERSATIONS"

The idea of "grand conversations" is the heart of the Questioning Cycle (Cecil, 1995, p. 24), the goal of which is for the teacher to begin with questions and to have as many of the students as possible respond to build their understanding of the concepts and topic being explored. Of course, during the process, the intent is for students to also ask their own questions to broaden the scope of the conversation and perhaps reach another learner in the class. Finally, through grand conversations, the teacher can continually assess student knowledge to ascertain the level of understanding. Teachers should recognize that just because a student uses a term does not necessarily mean that he or she has a comprehensive knowledge of its meaning. Sometimes the assessment reveals that students' knowledge is vague and imprecise (Graesser, 2006). Using the Questioning Cycle as a strategy helps the teacher in this assessment process. As students are engaged in well-considered Questioning Cycles that generate grand conversations, teachers can easily ascertain the extent of what the students have learned.

Teacher Reflection: The Learning Process

I have definitely noticed a change in how the children respond to questions. There are still some children who raise their hands right away, but more children are waiting, and I believe thinking, before they respond. I now try to ask higher-level questions even though I think that many of my students may not really be able to answer them. What I see happening is that they respond thoughtfully, attempting to reach the essence of my question. Their responses help me understand that you should ask the higher-level questions. Students will never be able to answer these basic questions if they don't interact with the higher-level ones. But I have not expected them necessarily to respond with higher-level ideas. What is the most amazing thing for me is that there are always one or two children who do respond with wonderful, creative answers. They teach me so much all the time. I am growing in my questioning skills and knowledge of the process. More importantly, I also am growing in my faith in children. From listening to their responses, I have learned that they can do far more than I expect. If I have high expectations, they meet them every time.

—5th-grade teacher

Moreover, when students recognize that the teacher is willing to help them elaborate on or rethink a response, they feel supported and gain confidence. As students of all abilities watch this happen, they become more willing to participate in discussions because they realize that classroom interactions are designed to generate thinking and build everyone's knowledge, that questions have real purposes other than embarrassing interrogations, and that their contributions will be bolstered by the teacher or peers whenever necessary.

An effective Questioning Cycle thus encourages creativity, experimentation, and cooperative thought. In the dynamic classrooms that result from its employment, it is common to hear students say things such as "I agree with Jennifer but I also see it a little differently," or "I agree with Jennifer but I think we need to think about this part, too." Follow-up questions and their responses encourage students to listen carefully and recognize what they know, what they are required to know, and why they think what they do. A heartening result is that in the same way that teachers probe student responses, teachers begin to hear a familiar refrain as their students say to one another, "Tell me why you think that."

Action Items

1. Have your students answer the following questions anonymously (so that they answer the questions freely).

   a. How do I feel when asked questions?
   b. When I respond to a question I . . .
   c. I ask questions when . . .
   d. The types of questions I prefer to answer are . . .
   e. The teacher asks me questions because . . .
   f. When a teacher asks me a follow-up question, I . . .
   g. When I answer a question . . .
   h. Teachers who ask a lot of questions . . .
   i. When other students are answering questions, I . . .
   j. What I learn from the teacher's questions . . .

2. Use the anecdotal sheet provided in Appendix D during your next discussion. See if it helps you better understand your students' thinking.

CHAPTER SEVEN

Using Responses to Re-Plan Instruction

A thinker sees his own actions as experiments and questions—as attempts to find out something.

—Friedrich Nietzsche

Re-planning questions and deciding on the direction for further instruction make up the last component of the Questioning Cycle. During this stage, the teacher has to decide whether the questions have been successful in building the concepts of the lesson. The teacher reflects and determines whether the questions have provided scaffolding for the learning and met the lesson's objectives. The teacher needs to decide which aspects of the interaction have been successful and which can guide the direction of the next questions. The teacher's focus is on what will help the students learn and perform more effectively.

What I have observed over the years is that once teachers tune into students' responses, they naturally begin to reflect more on the quality of those responses and the understanding they represent. Responses become assessment data, which then encourage teachers to re-plan and revise their lessons based on what students demonstrate they actually know. Further, teachers reflect on what fosters better interaction and development of the learning. Then teachers can undertake a number of steps to improve their performance and build students' responses from low-level cognitive skills (memorization) to greater powers of analysis and interpretation. All the information gathered enhances the lesson's content and enriches students' verbal and written responses. An email sent to me by social studies teacher John C., which I show in the Teacher Reflection that follows, drives this point home.

It is well known that students do not exist in a vacuum. They have a myriad of prior experiences that they can draw upon for information in order to respond to a question. Often, students do not understand this and teachers need to "encourage students to reflect on their world, to

---

Teacher Reflection: Reflection and Direction

It was a busy week. I managed to record four lessons and transcribed part of one. I am learning that I need to stay out of the way more; meaning less is more. I am noticing that I tend to use too much information in my questions rather than do what I did on the transcribed lesson I sent you. It's interesting hearing the lesson on tape. Also, I want to cut down on wasted time, which is probably what everyone realizes when they record themselves. The goal is becoming clearer—it is to build my students' thinking skills.

—8th-grade teacher

---

take stock of information gained just from living. Questions can be a link between the new information in the lesson and some content or situation with which students are already familiar" (Hunkins, 1995, p. 228). Questions can be a link between the new information in the lesson and some content or situation that students already know. A question that links the familiar with the unfamiliar engages students with their prior knowledge and enables teachers to determine the starting point for future lessons. As teachers reflect on the success of their questioning, they evaluate what they have learned from the links students have made with prior knowledge—and the links students have failed to make—and then use this information to plan the next step. Throughout this re-planning, teachers can avail themselves of a variety of systematic techniques that will support students' understanding of what constitutes a meaningful response to a question.

REVISING AND RE-PLANNING

In Chapter 6, we read about a teacher who used the following quote in a lesson with 4th-graders:

> I want to be beautiful but not so beautiful that a train moving in the sun like a metal peacock's glowing feather on tracks that are like stilts a thousand miles long laid down like a ladder up a flat mountain (wow!) seems dull. (Moss, 1993, p. 15)

As the teacher reflected upon the responses of her students, she realized that she had two different groups of students. One group had a good working knowledge of similes and the other did not. What both groups had in common was that they were interested in the use of similes and knowing more about them.

Thus, this 4th-grade teacher changed the direction of her lessons. Rather than having students begin to write poems with similes, she divided the class into the two groups. With the students who did not have a good knowledge of similes, she decided to read to them the book *Crazy Like a Fox: A Simile Story* (2008). After the students identified the simile they liked best, she had them create their own similes using the comparison items the author had used. With the other group of students, who were more familiar with similes, she followed a different procedure. She gave them the books *The Whales' Song* (1997) and *I'm as Quick as a Cricket* (1998) and organized them into working groups. Each group had to find as many similes in the story as possible and then determine why the author chose to use those comparisons. The groups' structure was set up with roles that included:

- *A Leader:* Who would ensure that the task got done
- *A Summarizer:* Who would provide a summary of what had been learned about similes
- *A Note-Taker:* Who would record what happened
- *A Visualizer:* Who would create a visual representation of the comparisons
- *A Simile Creator:* Who would list the similes and reasons why the author chose each comparison

With both groups, the teacher's approach was quite different from her initial lesson plans.

As another example of re-planning, let's return to the teacher in Chapter 6 whose 6th-grade class read *My Brother Sam Is Dead* (Collier & Collier, 1974). This teacher realized that some of her students were ready to read books that had open-ended conclusions. Therefore, in her literature circle groups, she began to offer more books that did not have formulaic endings. She found that there was a strong group of 6th-graders in her class who were ready to deal with more complex books such as *The Giver* by Lois Lowry (1993).

And finally, in Chapter 6, we met a teacher who recognized that her 1st-grade students did not realize that the change in temperature was creating the transition from summer to fall. Thus, as mentioned in that chapter, the teacher decided that her short- and long-term instructional goals should change. She decided to focus the rest of the unit on the attributes of fall (the fact that the days get cooler and shorter) to help her students understand the impact of temperature on the environment.

STRATEGIES THAT BUILD STUDENTS' RESPONSES

A key element in re-planning is to choose new strategies that help strengthen students' comprehension skills and enhance their capacities for thoughtful response. As we have discussed, responses to questions comprise literal, inferential, and metacognitive processes. Within these categories, there are subsets of questions that all demand different types of reasoning, and the thinking skill used to answer one question may not be the skill required for the next question.

Teaching Signal Words

For example, let's look at two possible questions a teacher might ask in a class:

1. Put the important events in the story in order.
2. What was the effect of the frost in the southern farm region?

These two questions require two different mental operations. The first question requires that a student select the main events in the story and then sequence them based on an accurate recollection of facts (dates). The second question requires the student to perceive a cause-and-effect relationship in order to respond appropriately. This may seem obvious to an adult reader, but for students it may not be apparent.

In one class, several 3rd-grade students responded to the question on frost by saying that the effect was that "it got colder." In this case, the teacher revised his lessons and coached the students to recognize that there are words in each question that can affect or guide the information required in a response. In his next lesson with the group, he had the students list the effects of cold weather. The group then reconsidered the effect of frost on southern farms.

The object, of course, is not just to get better answers to particular questions; it is to help students learn to apply the right approach. When a teacher realizes that students are missing signal words, as shown in the above example, the teacher should alert the students to the thinking skills necessary to answer that type of question. There are many signal words, and some are content-dependent.

For example, mathematical problems often contain signal words that indicate the direction for solving the problem. In one 1st-grade class, the teacher posed this problem: "James had seven pencils and found two more. How many pencils does James have?" When several students responded "seven," the teacher realized that the students needed to understand the words indicating that the operation of addition should take place. The class had been working with word problems, but the teacher now saw that she should support the students in recognizing that "found" in this context means "add." Working collaboratively with the students, the teacher generated a list of words that can mean "add," some of which were math-dependent and others that crossed into different content areas. Students began to realize that such words serve as a signal about what to do in a word problem.

Cathy Collins Block has added to our resources for teaching signal words. In her book *Teaching Comprehension* (2004), she includes a chart on cue or signal words to help guide students' responses. For example, the list includes words that indicate when students need to make a simple list of words, compare and contrast, respond with a cause-effect, draw a conclusion, and create a time sequence. Having a list of signal words gives students a starting point for their thinking when solving a difficult problem. Teachers, for their part, should use students' responses to determine whether the students understand the concepts and then to decide if they can use the opportunity to help students develop their thinking skills.

Teaching Specific Thinking Skills

Mr. T., a 7th-grade teacher, tried to engage in hypothetical thinking with his class, but he found that students became confused. He therefore revised his plan to ensure that all students understood what mental operation had to be performed to answer hypothetical questions. He realized that he had to review with the students the idea that a hypothesis is a guess or a possible reason that something happens or might occur. Mr. T. then planned a series of examples of what kind of thinking process might produce a hypothesis.

Since the class was working on a unit on erosion, Mr. T. then asked the students to create a hypothesis of their own about the causes of erosion in their local beaches (based upon their prior knowledge). He explained that a hypothesis must be:

1. based on real evidence (preferably gathered by the students themselves)
2. logical, relevant, and a contribution to the concepts that are being discussed
3. stated in a clear and simple manner

As the lesson progressed, the students began to create good hypotheses about erosion. These included:

Rainstorms cause erosion to land near oceans.
Rainstorms cause mountain erosion over extended time.
When erosion happens, the land does not disappear. It may become
    redistributed to nearby land.
Storm waves cause erosion to the coast.

From these hypotheses, Mr. T. realized that the students did have some knowledge of erosion and that one student seemed to understand the accretion that can take place during erosion. This led Mr. T. to a further revision of his plans. He decided that he could easily skip over the first two lessons that he had planned about the content, even though he had to spend more time on hypothetical questions. In this way, he saved himself valuable classroom instructional time.

What we see in this example is that the teacher taught a thinking skill, and as he was doing it, he assessed the responses to determine the further direction of the skill and the content he was teaching. These types of techniques help students realize that it is not sufficient to provide an answer that just pops into their heads; instead, they have to *do* something to make the information come together and be connected logically to the discussion and concept.

Teacher Reflection: Students' Questions

We have been working on questioning for a while in my class. I read a book to my students. After reading the story, I had students write questions about the book. Then, I separated my students into groups to answer each other's questions and decide on their group's best question to ask the whole class. The class answered the questions as I recorded their responses using a semantic map. Each group also provided the class with an explanation of why they thought that question was the best question. While we have only been working on modeling and coaching responses for a short time, I was impressed by their thinking and how they responded to questions. The coaching has really made a difference. More importantly, the questions that the students developed were a window into their comprehension of the story. It helps me decide which comprehension strategy I need to continue to work on with these students.

—5th-grade teacher

Figure 7.1. Questions and Thinking

Questions	Thinking Skill Required
Identify the . . .	Noticing and clarifying the details or attributes
Describe or explain . . .	Giving details and telling attributes
How are they alike or different?	Creating groups with attributes
Retell the story giving . . .	Sequencing the events
What is the main idea?	Combining/transforming data
What is your conclusion?	Grouping ideas and transforming them
How would you compare . . .	Creating a relationship
Predict the outcome . . .	Sequencing and transforming data given the known
Match these . . .	Comparing attributes of items and groups
Judge the success . . .	Creating and evaluating based on criteria

Working collaboratively, teachers and students can create a chart of different types of questions and the thinking skills needed for each. (See Figure 7.1 for an example.) This becomes a more effective strategy when the teacher has been engaged in re-planning and refocusing the discussion. Students realize that the teacher is supporting them in building their ability to respond to questions and that they, too, need to be involved in the planning process. Based on the question, they need to plan how they will respond.

Modeling Metacognition

Teachers can model ways to develop responses by demonstrating how they themselves reflect on conversations, questions, and ideas. Whenever such modeling occurs, students are afforded a deeper perception of thinking, learning, and content vocabulary. In particular, a teacher can engage students in metacognition by first explaining the process and then demonstrating to students how they can coordinate and integrate their thinking and better understand what they are learning. As I mentioned in an earlier chapter, metacognition is a strategy that helps students plan, monitor, and evaluate their thinking. More important, when students share their responses, they give teachers insight into what they are learning.

A simple activity to begin this process can be performed at the end of the day when a teacher asks students to think about what they have learned during the day and either write about it or draw it (1st-graders do a great job illustrating what they have learned). Some primary teachers divide a sheet of paper into five sections and have the children end their day by drawing the most important thing they have learned that day. On Friday, the youngsters take the sheet home to share with their parents. This activity is a good way to get students to reflect on their day and what has been learned. The following examples demonstrate the kinds of information that students share in their reflection.

> *1st Grade:* Today, I learned about the brain. It helps me think.
>
> *2nd Grade:* I had a good day today because I learned a lot. I learned that you have to read things more than one time; otherwise, you might misunderstand the question.
>
> *3rd Grade:* I learned what *lopsided* means. It's cool to know a new word.
>
> *4th Grade:* Wow! What a day I had today. I learned about something in math that I never heard of before. It was about circumference and diameters. I learned a formula to be able to measure circumferences of a circle.
>
> *5th Grade:* In science class I learned about why we put milk in the refrigerator. The refrigerator keeps it cold. The cold keeps the bacteria from reproducing in the milk. The cold keeps the milk from spoiling. If you don't put the milk in the refrigerator, the heat will make the bacteria reproduce more than if you keep it in the cold.
>
> *6th Grade:* I finished my book today and I wasn't happy. I like my books to have happy endings and this one did not. I learned that I like books to end the way they are supposed to end . . . happily ever after.
>
> *7th Grade:* The video helped me understand how glaciers are formed. I do better when I can actually see what I am supposed to be learning about in real life. How come we don't do more of this in our classes?
>
> *8th Grade:* I am so glad that we did not see *NightJohn* first. The book was actually better. I saw the characters differently. While the visual techniques were good, the writing was much better.

Besides being important for developing reflection, this process enables the teacher to hear what students think has been important or learned that day. These comments are another opportunity for the teacher to re-plan the direction for instruction the next day. One of the interesting things that I find when I do this in my undergraduate and graduate classes is that I always uncover misunderstanding about concepts and I can quickly go back and support the student in revising the faulty understanding.

In another article, I wrote, "Successful students seem to instinctively reflect on and regulate their learning, although they usually don't know why they do it or how it helps them. Less successful students seem almost unaware of the little voice in their heads and how they can use this voice to help themselves learn" (Fountain & Fusco, 1991, p. 255). To help students develop this little voice in their heads, teachers can use some of the questions shown in Figure 7.2 to encourage reflection and metacognitive development.

This type of metacognitive processing encourages students to become more active in the learning process and to develop a sense of responsibility. They begin to realize that they are supposed to be doing something in their heads when someone is speaking or when a question is addressed to them. When students are more reflective, they give their teachers more accurate information about what they know and what they don't know. This again leads to re-planning.

Figure 7.2. Metacognitive Questions

Question	Processes
What am I doing?	Create a focus (access short-term memory).
Why am I doing it?	Establish a purpose.
Why is it important?	Create reason(s) for doing it.
How/where does it fit in with what I already know?	Recognize appropriate context or interrelationships, look for similar relationships or connections.
What questions do I have?	Discover what is still unknown.

Source: Fountain & Fusco, 1991

RE-PLANNING:
REFLECTION, PRACTICE, AND PATIENCE

This chapter has focused mostly on the type of re-planning that occurs when a teacher reflects on an entire lesson and thinks about ways to re-direct the following lessons. Experienced teachers, though, learn to do a certain amount of re-planning on the spot. For instance, when a student responds to a question, the teacher may immediately recognize that the student needs more direction or that the student already has the information. In this case, the response may guide not only the follow-up question but also the direction of the rest of the lesson or unit.

Here are a few more examples of both types of re-planning. Some of these examples involve on-the-spot decisions by the teacher as he or she is interacting with the students. Others indicate that the teacher will work on this in the future.

> *The Whiskey Rebellion:* Students indicate that this was like the Boston Tea Party. (The teacher decides to teach the whole class about the Whiskey Rebellion.)
>
> *Fascism:* Students were discussing World War II and they indicated that this was Hitler's philosophy. When she asked who Mussolini was, students were not sure.
>
> *Subpoena:* Students indicated that you have to go to court if you get one. (The teacher decides to move ahead in the discussion and not teach this concept since he has many other aspects of the American court system to teach.)
>
> *Cells:* Students knew that living things are made up of thousands of tiny cells that transmit information to one another. (The teacher decides that students have some knowledge of cells but they need to explore the genetic aspects.)
>
> *Vertebrates:* Students knew that vertebrates are animals that have backbones and are different from invertebrates, which do not have them. (The teacher decides that students have a working relationship of the term *vertebrate* and its opposite. The lesson can move ahead rather than reviewing these concepts.)

Successful re-planning of instruction clearly takes time and experience. Sometimes the re-planning is in the moment, which requires practice and patience on the teacher's part. Other times, re-planning requires thoughtful reflection on the part of the teacher in order to systematically assess where students are in the learning process and how they can be moved ahead. The circumstances are different but the process is the same: thoughtful attention to students' knowledge and skills.

Action Items

1. After reading this chapter, which ideas do you think will be most beneficial to you? Why? How can you use the ideas?
2. Over the next 2 days, keep a list of all the times you have changed the direction of your teaching based on the response of your students. How many were on-the-spot decisions, and how many involved more extended reflection?

CHAPTER EIGHT

Students' Own Questions

He who asks questions, cannot avoid the answers.

—African Proverb

When teachers and students participate in the kind of "grand conversations" that this book has described, the class goes beyond simply responding to the teacher's questions. Students begin to ask questions of their own, and they feel more confident in doing so. This chapter will focus on that part of the process and how the teacher can encourage it.

Why is this important? In his book, *Developing More Curious Minds*, John Barell (2003) wrote that students become more inquisitive as a result of hearing and asking good questions. Barell goes on to assert that a good question reflects a genuine desire to find out about something, a deep feeling of wanting to know more than we already know. Questions, he believes, help us think and move beyond our immediate experience. When teachers encourage students to ask questions, they foster their inquisitiveness while at the same time gathering more information about their youngsters. Student-generated questions reveal what has been understood so far, which ideas are still perplexing, and which new ideas are still being considered. Equally important is the vibrant exchange that occurs when students answer one another's questions: Students realize that they, too, have good ideas and good questions and that thinking is not only the teacher's job. They feel empowered and the energy level of the class rises. Many students also realize that participation and authentic learning are their responsibility.

A real concern for teachers is raised in the *Mosaic of Thought*, in which authors Keene and Zimmermann (1997) lament the fact that children "who struggle as readers tend not to ask questions at any time as they read—before, during or after" (p. 100). Unfortunately, as we have seen, this is often true for many classroom situations. Students sit passively in the classroom while teachers "stand and deliver" the lessons. Students play the game: They know that if they are quiet and occasionally nod in agreement they will be rewarded. This type of instruction flies in the face of how knowledge is developed. Effective classroom dialogues in which students ask questions serve as one vehicle for individual construction of knowledge. Questions, especially student-generated ones, provide the teacher with the opportunity to assess and teach to the real needs of the students. Keene and Zimmermann feel that children learn more about one another from questions than from any answer they've stumbled upon.

Let's look at an example: In a kindergarten class, Theo, a student, has just completed showing his collection of glass fish and sharks. The following interaction occurs.

Questions in the Classroom: Asking Questions

TEACHER: Thank you, Theo, for bringing this in today. It adds beautifully to our discussion on life in the ocean. I will put these on my desk as a display for you all to look at. But please do not touch them. They are fragile.

JACQUELINE: What does *fragile* mean?

TEACHER: Does anyone know? (No responses.) Well, let's look one of them. What is it made of?

THEO: All of them are glass and can break.

JULIA: So does that mean that *fragile* means "breakable"?

TEACHER: Yes, it means it is breakable and, in this case, delicate. So we have to be careful of all the parts, like the tail on this shark because it can easily be broken. Notice how Theo brought them all in a special box.

JACQUELINE: Then *fragile* means "breakable," but then if something is not fragile, what do we call it?

TEACHER: That is another good question. Jackie, do you know?

JACQUELINE: If it can't break, then it is strong. Are *strong* and *fragile* opposites, like we said about *day* and *night*?

TEACHER: These are some interesting questions. Let's put the two words on our board. And then we will decide if *strong* and *fragile* are opposites.

When students feel free to ask questions, they are encouraged to be active in the classroom and to try out new ideas. Students can also question a previously taught area that they are not clear about, or ask questions because the idea does not coincide with their understanding. It is especially heartening to realize or rediscover that asking questions can be taught to children from an early age. In fact, very young children are very curious and ask many questions, usually beginning by imitating the teacher's behavior. Somehow this inquisitiveness seems to be lost as youngsters move along in the grades, but it can be reignited when teachers employ effective questioning strategies. When questions readily come from students—prompted by an encouraging teacher's behavior or modeling—it is a signal that they are comfortable in the classroom and engaged in learning. Our goal as teachers should be to foster students' curiosity and confidence so that they pepper us with animated and thoughtful questions.

When students ask their own questions, new avenues of intellectual exploration open for them. Michaels (1984) refers to this type of learning as *vertical construction*, a situation in which the teacher and the students collaborate to develop the concept that is being discussed. This speaks to the purpose of the Questioning Cycle: These collaborative interactions allow students to expand upon ideas and use more precise vocabulary in speaking and later in their writing (Roe & Ross, 2006). Such processes welcome all ideas. Diverse perspectives come together to give depth to the concepts that are being examined, and evidence is given to support the point being constructed.

Other educators support this perspective when they state that "when students have opportunities to ask their own questions, they are practicing habits of mind that can help them think, learn, and achieve at higher levels" and that they become more effective thinkers and learners as a result (Walsh & Sattes, 2005, p. 131).

Personally, I have learned from many years of teaching that when students are in a classroom where they can ask a genuine question, the environment fosters the following traits:

- Self-esteem
- Content vocabulary and communication skills
- Creativity
- Tolerance
- Divergent thinking
- Problem-solving skills
- Ability to deal with complexity
- Better attitudes toward school
- Motivation and self-direction
- Inquisitiveness

If students are engaged in a meaningful discussion, and divergent questions and multiple responses are a significant part of the experience, they behave differently. They seem to believe that questions are more valid because someone in their class actually wants to know something. Students become attentive when listening to the explanations of their peers, and they also build their ability to self-correct as they think about their responses or listen to those of their peers. The students learn that there is no right or wrong answer to an open-ended question. Thus, they recognize that the goal of questions is to broaden everyone's perspective, and are a way to build a shared conceptualization about the topic. Scaffolding of knowledge occurs because more than one idea and many details are added to the concept being discussed (Michaels, 1984).

Finally, students learn that whatever the situation, their asking a question is important to the teacher and their fellow students. They understand that by allowing their curiosity to flow, they help build the consciousness of the students who surround them.

TEACHING THE QUESTIONING PROCESS

Those who stress the need to encourage children to ask questions also advocate the benefits of training them *how* to ask these questions. One helpful way to do this is for the teacher to post a list of question words or Bloom's Taxonomy with the different categories of verbs in different colors, as shown below:

Blue = knowledge
Green = comprehension
Red = application
Purple = analysis
Yellow = synthesis
Orange = evaluation

By employing these colors, both the teacher and the students recognize when they are moving up and down the levels. Teachers can also create a list of starter statements or questions. These help students begin to verbalize their ideas, and teachers can also have their students add to these lists. Such a list might include the following phrases:

I was curious about . . .
The difference I noticed was . . .
The question I had was . . .
I see it differently . . .
There was a relationship . . .
What is problematic for me . . .
What was challenging . . .
I would judge it differently . . .
A plan that might have worked . . .

That triggered a different idea . . .
The information I needed was . . .

Another technique to build students' abilities to ask and answer questions is the notion of respondent-centered questions. With this strategy, the teacher builds the students' ability to communicate their ideas and information in standard ways. It enables students to:

1. explain details, sequence, main ideas, and themes
2. generate problem–solution sequences
3. assimilate dissimilar events into their own lives
4. express affective response and insights
5. justify and defend their positions
6. ask questions or react to responses (adapted from Block, 2004, p. 18)

I encourage teachers to place Block's list on a chart in the room and to refer to it during discussions. This type of support provides direction for students in the discussion. It also connects to the SOLO Taxonomy that we discussed in Chapter 6. It encourages students to elaborate on the responses. To Block's original list, I have added item number 6, which encourages students to also ask questions and become part of the inquiry process.

EXAMPLES OF ENCOURAGING THE QUESTIONING PROCESS

An easy place to begin encouraging students to use questioning skills in a classroom is during a read-aloud. The teacher can have students write down questions they have on sticky notes. As students listen to the story and as questions arise in the reading or they wonder about something, they jot down these thoughts and questions. Alternatively, the teacher can create a "Questions I Have" sheet that students can use to keep track of questions they have as a story is read to them.

The examples in Figures 8.1 and 8.2 come from elementary classrooms. Figure 8.1 is a 2nd-grade student's questions as the book *Strega Nona* (1975) is read in a class. Figure 8.2 illustrates the questions that a 4th-grade student had while listening to *The Lotus Seed* (1997). What we see from these student examples is a range of questions that show students' interests and ideas about the story. The teacher does not have to ask any questions because the students ask their own. In my experience with this type of activity, students love to ask their questions and are just as excited to respond to their peers' questions. I have heard children say during this type of session: "I didn't even think of that," or, "What made you think of that?" Once students have created their questions, they then work in groups. They determine which questions are most important and are still unanswered and then they bring these back to a whole-class discussion. This makes for a very interesting discussion, which is often student-led.

Figure 8.1. A 2nd-Grade Student's Questions on *Strega Nona*

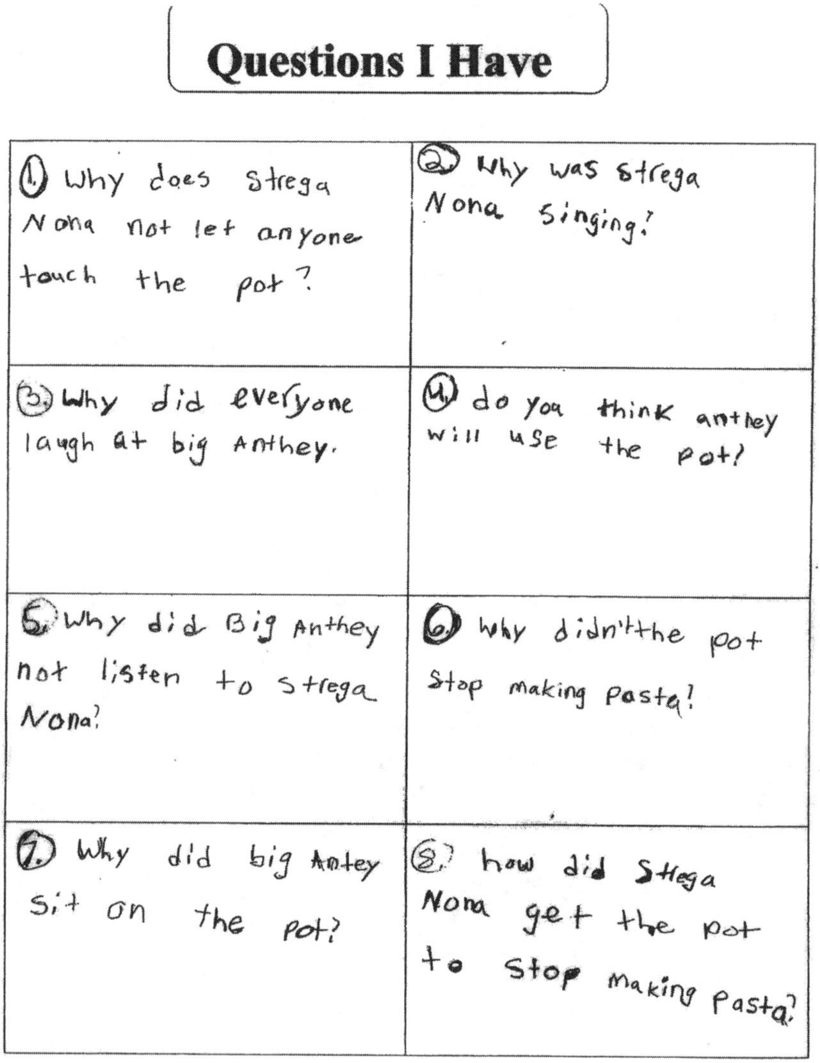

Questions I Have

1.) Why does Strega Nona not let anyone touch the pot?	2.) Why was Strega Nona Singing?
3.) Why did everyone laugh at big Anthey.	4.) do you think anthey will use the pot?
5.) Why did Big Anthey not listen to Strega Nona?	6.) Why didn't the pot Stop making Pasta?
7.) Why did big Antey sit on the pot?	8.) how did Strega Nona get the pot to Stop making Pasta?

Another resource is Stephanie Harvey's video *Strategy Instruction in Action* (Harvey & Goudvis, 2002), which illustrates students performing this task in an elementary classroom. It is a wonderful video to observe children creating their own questions regarding a book. I have even seen teachers show their own classes parts of the video to help their students

Figure 8.2. A 4th-Grade Student's Questions on *The Lotus Seed*

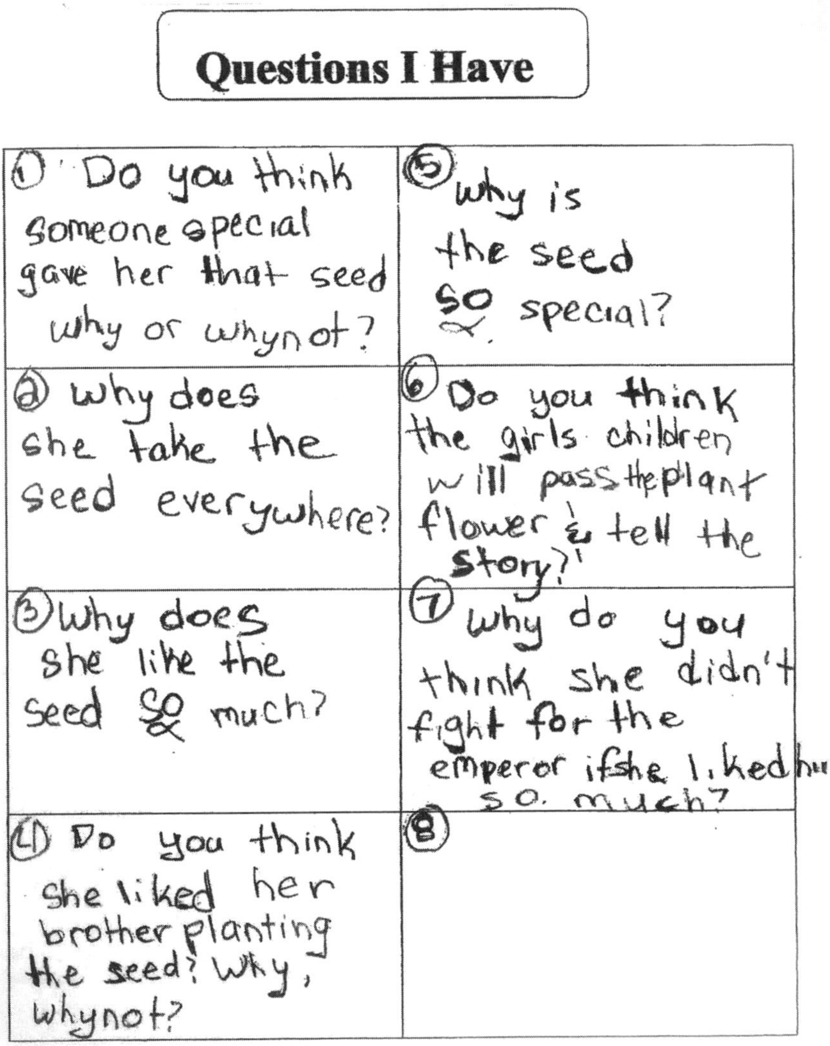

Questions I Have

① Do you think someone special gave her that seed why or why not?	⑤ why is the seed so special?
② why does she take the seed everywhere?	⑥ Do you think the girls children will pass the plant flower & tell the story?'
③ Why does she like the seed so much?	⑦ why do you think she didn't fight for the emperor if she liked her so much?
④ Do you think she liked her brother planting the seed? Why, why not?	⑧

understand their responsibility in listening and creating questions regarding a story.

These examples suggest that students can create logical questions that effectively connect to the learning. When students ask questions, teachers are provided with information that has been learned. Students have to think about what they are learning when they ask their questions. Catherine Cornbleth, in her article "Student Questioning as Learning Strategy," wrote, "there is compelling evidence that student questioning has many benefits":

- All students can be encouraged to ask productive or critical questions.
- The more questions a student asks in any one time period, the greater the probability that the questions will be higher level.
- Students become more actively engaged in classes where they are encouraged to ask their own questions. (Cornbleth, 1975, p. 219)

Students have a more sophisticated outlook toward learning and express that they have a better sense of their own knowledge when they are allowed to ask questions. They feel that their questions help them have a better sense of what they know. By listening to their peers' questions, they are also being made aware of other aspects of a topic. Teaching students to ask questions is another component of the Questioning Cycle.

Seen in this light, the use of the Questioning Cycle in a classroom is very satisfying for youngsters: They enjoy the ongoing dialogue with the teacher and their peers, they become involved with the discussion and even begin to spontaneously ask questions of their peers, and they begin to anticipate these types of discussions as an important part of the lesson. Students recognize that they have a real role in their classroom. Because they are more involved and engaged in classroom dialogue, they often become more effective in their preparation. They come to respect the commitment of the teacher and their peers in the learning process. Whatever their ages, students want to be heard, and asking relevant questions is an opportunity to be heard and to help foster a community of learners.

Over the course of the school year, the teacher who gradually introduces the notion of students asking questions and uses their responses to direct instruction finds that the class has an inviting atmosphere, as I have mentioned in the previous chapter. It is important for the teacher to provide appropriate guided practice until students understand how and when to ask questions that can build their thinking and learning experiences. When this happens, teachers and students become a team working to discover important concepts and skills that will build knowledge for everyone.

Teacher Reflection: Asking More Questions

In my experience of teaching questioning to my 4th-grade students, I discovered that they were eager to learn strategies that would help them to ask good, thought-provoking questions. Although there were a few students who were pessimistic about our class study on Bloom's Taxonomy, the majority of students showed enthusiasm and excitement to use the Bloom categories and verbs as a resource to help them ask good questions. As a class, we discussed the types of questions we could ask to help increase student conversation in our discussions. The results have been so interesting. Students do ask more questions and now sometimes tell me they have a higher-level question to ask that is better than my question. I feel that teaching my students strategies for asking questions will help them with every aspect of their social and educational lives.

—4th-grade teacher

Action Items

1. Using your content-area word wall or a vocabulary chart from a thematic unit, have students generate a list of questions related to the topic you are studying. After the students have finished writing their questions, engage them in a discussion on higher-order thinking and have them analyze their questions. (You may want to merely use literal and inferential questions as a first step in this process.) What types of questions did they ask? What is their understanding of the different levels of questions?

2. Teach a lesson on any topic. After you have completed the lesson, have the students write three questions that you could use if you were going to give them a test on the topic. Review the students' questions and use the information to determine what students learned from the lesson. What types of questions did they write? How do their questions relate to the types of questions that you ask?

CHAPTER NINE

The Impact of Questions

The important thing is not to stop questioning.

—Albert Einstein

The Questioning Cycle creates an atmosphere in the classroom that values the fact that knowledge is actively constructed in many different ways, and it respects the use of language and conversation as a way to develop thinking. This Questioning Cycle classroom environment demonstrates an important tenet: Listening to others and respecting the ideas of others is beneficial for all members of the classroom community. All students have had the opportunity to become aware, implicitly as well as explicitly, that they are becoming better thinkers and problem-solvers because their ideas are acknowledged and often expanded upon by others. Students in a Questioning Cycle classroom report that they learn to share ideas, see details, make better choices, and evaluate new situations. They appear to be more aware of their thinking, seeing it not simply as a step-by-step process but as an attitude of increased alertness and responsiveness. Questioning strategies also encourage students to think collaboratively with their peers. They discover that fellow learners can view a concept differently and, moreover, that their combined information can create a greater and more intriguing whole. They recognize, too, that such collaboration can occur across different content areas.

In a Questioning Cycle classroom, students are encouraged to research ideas and questions that develop as they discuss topics. Motivated by their interests, students are more likely to engage in the active construction of knowledge, to make real connections, and to remember what they learn. As noted earlier in this book, when both teachers and students ask authentic questions, new depths of learning for all students can be explored. An example of this occurred in a 4th-grade class when a student asked the teacher questions about the Native American custom of using dream catchers as part of their culture. The student then asked, "Why don't we use them today to help young children with nightmares?" His question made the lesson content more immediate and relevant, both for himself and his classmates.

Because the Questioning Cycle supports every aspect of cognitive development as well as the acquisition and use of language, teachers who have used this method describe a wide range of benefits for all students, including students who have been having difficulties in learning. For example, all students realize that they must monitor their own thinking to determine whether they understand the concepts that are being discussed (Baumann, Jones, & Seifert-Kessell, 1993). Students also benefit from the Questioning Cycle in the following ways:

- They come to recognize, implicitly as well as explicitly, that as "co-inquirers" they have a responsibility to participate in the discussion and to ask questions when necessary.
- They build their listening and oral language skills because they feel encouraged to participate in meaningful communication.
- They experience and respond to the thinking of their peers.
- They come to understand how they solve problems in each of the different subjects. They get to hear that the way their peers respond to a question in math, for example, may be different from their own responses to a question in literature.
- They get the message that we are *all* collecting information; our ideas are interesting; no one has all the answers; our thought processes are valued; and concepts have depth and breadth.
- The students' perception of the teacher changes: They perceive that the teacher is not the sole repository of knowledge but the facilitator of knowledge development.
- The students are reminded, within the social nature of these interactions and dialogues, that they are real conversationalists who have knowledge that is worth sharing, and that they can fend for themselves in a conversation and contribute to the group's knowledge.

These insights help students realize that they can become independent learners and contributing members of a classroom community (Strickland, Galda, & Cullinan, 2004).

An example of this profound exchange occurred in an art class in which the teacher asked students to analyze a painting and give their opinion about the artist's purpose in creating the work. Students first wrote about their reactions and then shared their different perspectives in a discussion. The teacher asked questions, followed up the students' responses, and asked more questions. At the end of the class, the teacher asked the students what they had learned. One student said he discovered that we all have so many different ideas, and he then went on to add,

"What I really learned is that from other people's ideas, I make different connections that I never would have thought about before because I didn't see it that way."

These types of experiences naturally develop in an environment where questioning is effectively used and the teacher has made a decision to be student-centered. A quote from one educator underscores this observation: "The most important belief related to teachers' work is that attention should be placed on students' learning and not on what should be taught. The most critical belief related to individuals themselves is that changing and improving is a journey and not a series of events" (Martin-Kniep, 2000, p. 99). When a school commits itself to employing the Questioning Cycle, it also commits itself to the idea that teaching students—not just facts, not just lesson content—is the heart of quality instruction. These techniques can thus be reinforced in all disciplines, from the classroom to the gymnasium, and children can learn to thrive as thinkers and as people.

TOOLS FOR TEACHERS

Those teachers who choose to employ the Questioning Cycle face a demanding (but not entirely daunting) task. They recognize that they need to reflect on their instruction and the performance of their students to determine whether students are achieving at their best performance levels and therefore becoming proficient. Further, they have to support students as they acquire literal, inferential, and metacognitive skills. They need to be models of different thought processes: exploring problem-solving, delving into author strategies, creating a scientific hypothesis, and so on.

One tool to begin implementing the Questioning Cycle, mentioned earlier, is an anecdotal sheet on which student responses during a discussion are recorded, allowing the teacher to see whether students are:

- Analyzing the questions before responding
- Organizing the information to create a response that is meaningful
- Noting significant ideas that have been stated and using them to build their responses
- Correlating information that has been given to create a more elaborated response
- Posing appropriate questions that forward the discussion
- Responding more critically and having evidence for their opinions
- Providing responses that demonstrate they have interpreted the information and have created a new idea

Teacher Reflection: Listening and Assessing

When I am working with small groups, I always have felt comfortable with using open-ended questions in a discussion environment. Students discuss back and forth and readily answer questions. After videoing my classroom, I realized that I successfully used this approach with my whole-class discussions. It is interesting to hear how students interact in this situation and that good conversation develops out of it. On the other hand, because I am modeling how to ask a question or respond to one, less assertive children seem more willing to participate. I didn't think this would happen but my video proved it works. During the lesson, I was able to see again who participated. As I watched, it made me think about other ways I can bring all students into the lesson. However, now that I am more aware of the differences in how I handle small and large groups' lessons, I can better adapt myself to the needs of my students and figure out the best way to teach in each of these situations.

Another area I reflected on was assessment. I realized that I am able to pay attention to my students and assess certain things instantly and to adapt myself during the lesson. This allows me to find different ways to question them and involve them in the lesson. Another success was that I recognize what students were saying and understand when they had grasped a concept. This allowed me to quickly move on. It is important to be able to assess students during a lesson, not just at the end. I previously felt I was not as capable and would second-guess myself. After viewing this video, I see that I am starting to do it more naturally. I am listening to the responses to my questions and asking follow-up questions that assist my students in thinking more deeply about the question and its concept.

—6th-grade teacher

By using this tool, the teacher can determine the direction for future instruction for each student in the classroom. The teacher can then employ the Questioning Cycle to support what individual students need to learn or explore about a topic.

Another way that teachers can assess the efficacy of their planned Questioning Cycle is to think about the following:

- Do I use teacher- and student-generated questions in all subjects and with all concepts?
- What do I do to engage all students all of the time?

- How do I demonstrate that I appreciate and respect all authentic responses?
- Do all students use their own language to respond, or do I finish or restate their answers?
- Do I provide real feedback to responses? How do I know that this is true?
- What are the indicators that I have created a community of learners?
- Do I continuously adjust my teaching based on what my students' responses tell me, or do I go on with my planned lesson?
- How do I measure the gains that my students are achieving?
- How do I document daily learning and measure this against the content that needs to be taught?

Although, at times, the avenues that a student may explore may appear not to be the right direction, the fact that the teacher encourages the youngster to explore pays great dividends. As teachers allow students to explore tangents, students demonstrate that they are interested in understanding concepts, acknowledging that perhaps there is more information and even an alternative perspective to uncover (even a relevant perspective that the teacher might not have considered). Students can feel more responsible for the integrity of ideas in the classroom. They can begin to grasp the idea that learning is a multifaceted process and that, as they learn, they must simultaneously be critical observers and active participants. They come to understand that their knowledge base cannot rest only on their textbooks but can be expanded by their peers, the teacher's instruction, and an array of curriculum resources.

Consider using the checklist in Figure 9.1 as a quick reference to ensure that your own discussions are lively and productive.

THE IMPACT OF QUESTIONS: FINAL THOUGHTS

The purpose of this book has been to provide both beginning and experienced teachers with methods to create an exhilarating exchange with students and to provide understanding of the benefits of employing the Questioning Cycle.

What I have seen in classrooms that use the Questioning Cycle are teachers who are more actively engaged in helping students develop their knowledge. They begin by describing how they themselves develop a richer understanding of the different concepts they teach in all the

Figure 9.1. A Checklist for Evaluating Your Use of the Questioning Cycle

Questions	Sometimes	Always
Did my questions build conversations with my students?		
Did my questions recognize students' knowledge background?		
Did I focus my questions to relate to the essential questions in my lessons?		
Did I use a range of types of questions?		
Did I recognize and equally engage all students?		
Did I avoid calling on one group of students more than another?		
Did I allow for students' questions?		
Did I allow for student-to-student interactions?		
Did I avoid using questions as a discipline method?		

subjects. Most apparent is the realization that when they start using better questions in their discussion, students are more willing to explore alternative perspectives, including those that teachers have not even considered. More and more, I hear from teachers that they, or their students, have to check on ideas or information that students ask about or state in a discussion, and their subsequent responses are more original and complex. One teacher indicated that in the past, she had dismissed responses that were not in her head; however, now that she has listened to tapes of her interactions with students, she considers the ideas that students suggest and asks them to check for the accuracy or possibility of the idea. This had never happened before. Students become more enthusiastic about classroom participation and learning itself because they recognize that ideas are being explored and they can have different opinions—and that these are not only valued but sometimes create a shift in the direction of the instruction. This, in turn, builds the confidence of teachers, who inevitably feel more competent about their instructional abilities and heartened by the growth they perceive in their students.

Teachers also discover that questioning strategies provide an alternative to testing because they can more spontaneously evaluate the strengths and weaknesses of students. In classroom discussions, students know that

---

Teacher Reflection: Using Higher-Level Questions

I noticed that when I asked lower-level questions, I received very shallow responses from my students. When I asked high-level questions, the students put more thought and effort into their answers. I also found that when the students are asked high-level questions, they start to become more interested in what they are learning. Therefore, they think of questions of their own that they want to ask me. I have them ask the class and we get great answers. Sometimes they have ideas that I did not think of for that question.

I have been doing lessons with my students about World War II. The more in-depth I got with my questions, the more excited the students became and wanted to learn about it. They also made connections to World War I and the Civil War, which was very exciting to me. It surprises me about how well they can think.

—5th-grade teacher

---

they must sustain their reasoning and base their responses on evidence, essential skills that allow them to perform successfully in a broad range of contexts. Testing will still be necessary at times, and because students have been in a classroom where they are required to interact with questions, their acquired skills are readily transferred to paper-and-pencil activities, including standardized tests.

Finally, administrators and teachers who choose to employ the Questioning Cycle should remember that the process is demanding but immensely revitalizing. At the heart of good classroom instruction is the responsibility to continually engage students in learning, and to coach them as they attempt to implement their new skills. However halting or awkward the process may be (for teachers and students alike), the result is a learning environment that is active, dynamic, stimulating, and challenging. Sometimes it can even be exhilarating, but it is rarely dull or alienating. From this thought-provoking environment, teachers hope to encourage students to become curious, lively, courteous, and accomplished. We hope that when they leave our classrooms, they will still ask questions as vibrant seekers of knowledge, eager thinkers who will be constantly engaged in the discovery and creation of the world they live in.

Consider these final Questions in the Classroom from a 3rd-grade classroom.

Questions in the Classroom: Using Strategies

TEACHER: That was an interesting idea. How did you come up with your answer?

KRIS: I am using the tricks that you showed us. I even use them at home when my mom or dad asks me a question.

TEACHER: What do you mean, "tricks"?

KRIS: I think that all the ways you show us how to answer questions are like magic because when I use them I get better ideas and answers. I see that happening with other kids in the class, too. So they are tricks.

TEACHER: You could call them tricks or you could call them strategies. Why do you think they help you? And did you use a specific strategy when you answered the question?

KRIS: I knew that I had to think back on stuff we had learned and I remembered an example I saw when I was researching my report on turtles. I copied that idea and used it with this. You told us that we can model our ideas on other ideas.

In this 3rd-grade child's perspective, understanding how to answer questions is like magic! I will not make that claim myself, but I do believe that the Questioning Cycle can transform a classroom learning experience in almost miraculous ways. I believe from my many experiences that teachers recognize that they now have a new control over their instructional program and they delight in this accomplishment. That in itself is a miracle.

> The principal goal of education is to create people who are capable of doing new things, not simply of repeating what other generations have done—people who are creative, inventive, and discoverers. The second goal of education is to form minds which can be critical, can verify, and not accept everything they are offered.
>
> —Jean Piaget

Action Items

1. Over the next week, as you work with students, observe your classroom. What evidence do you have in your daily instruction that shows high levels of thinking in your students?
2. Consider Figure 9.2, which is a partial checklist of behaviors that students can develop through the use of the Questioning Cycle. Add other behaviors based on your own teaching style.

Figure 9.2. Attitudes and Skills That My Students Can Accomplish

	Usually	Sometimes	Needs to Develop
Respects wait time			
Able to listen carefully in discussions			
Contributes to a discussion			
Respects peers' questions			
Asks questions during a discussion			
Provides evidence for opinions and ideas			

3. Find a committed partner with whom you can work on the Questioning Cycle. Have your partner observe you in your classroom, and then do the same for him or her. Focus on your questioning techniques. Then select one strategy from this book that you would like to use in a lesson. Teach the lesson. After the lesson is completed, discuss what you have observed. How were the students affected by this lesson? Was there any reaction to the new strategy?

4. Use the Learning Guide in Appendix E with your students to begin to support their active engagement in the learning process. Ask them for their reactions.

Notes from Bloom's *Taxonomy* of *Educational Objectives*

Knowledge: "Involves the recall of specific facts, the recall of methods and processes or the recall of a pattern, structure or setting" (Bloom, 1987, pp. 202–203). This category involves knowledge in areas such as terminology, facts, names, conventions, and sequences.

Comprehension: "This involves the lowest level of understanding. It refers to a type of understanding such that the individual knows what is being communicated and can make use of the material or idea being communicated without necessarily relating it to other material or seeing its fullest implication" (Bloom, 1987, p. 204). This category involves interpreting statements, summarizing a communication, translating information, and recognizing conclusions. These are at the literal level and the information is stated.

Application: This category moves to the inferential level. "The use of abstractions in particular and concrete situations. The abstractions may be in the form of general ideas, rules of procedures or generalized methods. This category involves the ability to use technical principles, ideas, and theories which must be remembered and applied" (Bloom, 1987, p. 205). It involves applying information from one situation to another.

Analysis: "The breakdown of communication into its constituent elements or parts such that the relative hierarchy of ideas is made clear and/or the relations between the ideas expressed are made explicit. This category involves the ability to recognize assumptions; distinguishing facts from hypotheses and comprehending interrelationships among the ideas" (Bloom, 1987, p. 205). The ability to separate the parts from the whole and understand their relationship is essential in this category.

Synthesis: "The putting together of elements and parts so as to form a whole. This involves the process of working with pieces, parts, elements, etc., and arranging and combining them in such a way as to constitute a pattern or structure clearly not there before" (Bloom, 1987, p. 206).

Evaluation: "Judgments about the value of materials and methods for given purposes. Quantitative and qualitative judgments about the extent to which material and methods satisfy criteria. Use of a standard of appraisal. The criteria may be determined by students or by others. This involves the ability to assess, comprehend and judge by external standards" (Bloom, 1987, p. 207). The criteria for assessment can be subjective or objective.

Notes from Gronland's
Stating Objectives
for Classroom Instruction

The following verbs are found in the lists in Norman E. Gronland's (1985) book. He uses these to show how to use the taxonomy for the cognitive domain. In his book, he has written a more comprehensive list for teachers to use with their writing and questioning (see Gronland, 1985, p. 37).

Knowledge: Defines, describes, identifies, labels, lists, matches, names, outlines, reproduces, selects, states

Comprehension: Converts, defends, distinguishes, estimates, explains, extends, generalizes, gives, examples, infers, paraphrases, predicts, rewrites, summarizes

Application: Changes, converts, demonstrates, discovers, manipulates, modifies, operates, predicts, prepares, produces, relates, shows, solves, uses

Analysis: Breaks down, diagrams, differentiates, discriminates, distinguishes, identifies, illustrates, infers, outlines, points out, relates, selects, separates, subdivides

Synthesis: Categorizes, combines, compiles, composes, creates, devises, designs, explains, generates, modifies, organizes, plans, rearranges, reconstructs, relates, reorganizes, revises, rewrites, summarizes, tells, writes

Evaluation: Appraises, compares, concludes, contrasts, criticizes, describes, discriminates, explains, justifies, interprets, relates, summarizes, supports

APPENDIX C

Questions to Use in Lessons

Question	Students Who Responded
Compare and Contrast	
Clarification	
Change	
Point of View	
Feelings	
Preferences	
Summary	

Question	Students Who Responded
Clarification	
Evaluation	
Consequence	
Relational	
Elaboration and/or Extension	
Give an Example	
Descriptive Information	
What If?	
How Come?	
I Wonder	

Anecdotal Form

Concepts Being Taught _____

Student Names	Knowledge or Comments Made During Discussion

Learning Guide

List new words.

List two important ideas you learned.
1.   2.

Write two questions you have about what we are learning.
1.   2.

Summarize how this information fits into what you have been learning.

References

Alvermann, D. E., Dillon, D. R., & O'Brien, D. G. (1987). *Using discussion to promote reading comprehension.* Newark, DE: International Reading Association.

Anderson, L. W., & Krathwohl, D. R. (Eds.). (2001). *Taxonomy of learning, teaching, and assessing: A revision of Bloom's taxonomy of educational objectives.* New York: Addison Wesley Longman.

Armstrong, T. (1994). *Multiple intelligences in the classroom.* Alexandria, VA: Association for Supervision and Curriculum Development.

Armstrong, W. H. (1969). *Sounder.* New York: Harper & Row.

Atwood, V. A., & Wilen, W. W. (1991, March). Wait time and effective social studies instruction: What can research in science education tell us? *Social Education, 55,* 179–181.

Avi. (1979). *Night journey.* New York: Scholastic Book Service.

Barell, J. (2003). *Developing more curious minds.* Alexandria, VA: Association for Supervision and Curriculum Development.

Barnette, J., Orletski, S., Sattes, B., & Walsh, J. (1995, April). *Wait-time: Effective and trainable.* Paper presented at the annual meeting of the American Educational Research Association, San Francisco, CA. (ERIC Document Reproduction Service No.ED383706)

Baumann, J. F., Jones, L. A., & Seifert-Kessell, N. (1993). Using think alouds to enhance children's comprehension monitoring abilities. *The Reading Teacher, 47*(3), 184–193.

Biggs, J. B., & Collis, K. F. (1982). *Evaluating the quality of learning.* New York: Academic Press.

Block, C. C. (2004). *Teaching comprehension.* New York: Pearson.

Block, C. C., & Israel, S. E. (2004). The ABCs of performing highly effective think-alouds. *The Reading Teacher, 58*(2). Newark, DE: International Reading Association.

Bloom, B. S. (1987). *Taxonomy of educational objectives: Book 1 Cognitive domain.* White Plains, NY: Longman.

Brooks, J. G. (2002). *Schooling for life.* Alexandria, VA: Association for Supervision and Curriculum Development.

Bunting, E. (1989). *The Wednesday surprise.* New York: Houghton Mifflin.

Cecil, N. L. (1995). *The art of inquiry.* Winnipeg, MB, Canada: Peguis Publishers.

Christenbury, L., & Kelly, P. P. (1983). *Questioning a path to critical thinking*. Urbana, IL: ERIC and National Council of Teachers of English.

Collier, J. L., & Collier, C. (1974). *My brother Sam is dead*. New York: Four Winds Press.

Cornbleth, C. (1975). Student questioning as a learning strategy. *Educational Leadership, 33*, 219–222.

Costa, A. L. (2001). Teacher behaviors that enable students thinking. In A. L. Costa (Ed.), *Developing minds* (pp. 194–206). Alexandria, VA: Association for Supervision and Curriculum Development.

Danielson, C. (2007). *Enhancing professional practice*. Alexandria, VA: Association for Supervision and Curriculum Development.

DePaola, T. (1975). *Strega Nona*. New York: Simon & Schuster.

Dewey, J. (1991). *How we think*. Amherst, NY: Prometheus Books. (Original work published 1910)

Dillon, J. T. (1990). *The practice of questioning*. London and New York: Routledge.

Erlauer, L. (2003). *The brain-compatible classroom: Using what we know about learning to improve teaching*. Alexandria, VA: Association for Supervision and Curriculum Development.

Fountain, G., & Fusco, E. (1991). A strategy to support metacognitive processing. In A. L. Costa (Ed.), *Developing minds* (pp. 255–258). Alexandria, VA: Association for Supervision and Curriculum Development.

Fusco, E. (1983). *The relationship between children's cognitive level of development and their responses to literature*. Doctoral dissertation, Hofstra University, Hempstead, NY.

Gardner, H. (1991). *The unschooled mind*. New York: Basic Books.

Gardner, H. (2006). *Multiple intelligences: New horizons*. New York: Basic Books.

Garland, S. G. (1997). *The lotus seed*. New York: Sandpiper.

Graesser, A. C. (2006). Views from a cognitive scientist: Cognitive representations underlying discourse are sometimes social. *Discourse Studies, 8*, 59–66.

Gronlund, N. E. (1985). *Stating objectives for classroom instruction*. New York: Macmillan.

Guilhas, R. *Perhaps*. Available at http://www.netpoets.com/poems/friends/0271001.htm

Harvey, S., & Goudvis, A. (2002). *Strategy instruction in action* [video]. Portland, ME: Stenhouse Publishers.

Hughes, C. (1987/1988). All students can learn to be better thinkers. *Oklahoma Middle Level Education Association Journal*, pp. 1–7.

Hunkins, F. P. (1995). *Teaching thinking through effective questions* (2nd ed.). Norwood, MA: Christopher-Gordon.

Kamii, C., Manning M., & Manning, G. (Eds.). (1991). *Early literacy: A constructivist foundation for whole language*. Washington, DC: National Education Association.

Keene, E. O., & Zimmermann, S. (1997). *Mosaic of thought*. Portsmouth, NH: Heinemann.

Keirsey, D., & Bates, M. (1978). *Please understand me*. Delmar, CA: Prometheus Nemesis Books.

Kellogg, S. (1999). *Aster Aardvark's alphabet adventure*. New York: Mulberry Books.

King, A., & Rosenshine, B. (1993). Effects of guided cooperative-questioning on children's knowledge construction. *Journal of Experimental Education, 6*, 127–148.

Leedy, L. (1994). *Messages in the mailbox: How to write a letter*. New York: Holiday House.

Leedy, L. (2008). *Crazy like a fox: A simile story*. New York: Holiday House.

Lowery, L. F. (2005). *Asking effective questions*. Berkeley: University of California.

Lowery, L. F. (1989). *Thinking and learning*. Pacific Grove, CA: Midwest Publications.

Lowry, L. F. (1993). *The giver*. New York: Houghton Mifflin.

Ma, W. (2006, Fall/Winter). Sharing perspectives and practices. *Excelsior: Leadership in teaching and learning, 1*(1), 29–35.

Martin-Kniep, G. O. (2000). *Becoming a better teacher*. Alexandria, VA: Association for Supervision and Curriculum Development.

Marzano, R. J., & Kendall, J. S. (2007). *The new taxonomy of educational objectives*. Thousand Oaks, CA: Corwin Press.

Marzano, R. J., Pinkering, D. J., & Pollock, J. E. (2001). *Classroom instruction that works: Research-based strategies for increasing student achievement*. Alexandria, VA: Association for Supervision and Curriculum Development.

McTighe, J., & Wiggins, G. (1999). *The understanding by design handbook*. Alexandria, VA: Association for Supervision and Curriculum Development.

Myers, I. B. (1985). *Gifts differing*. Palo Alto, CA: Consulting Psychologists Press.

Michaels, S. (1984). Listening and responding: Hearing the logic of children's classroom narratives. *Theory into Practice, 23*, 218–224.

Moss, T. (1993). *I want to be*. New York: Penguin Books.

National Institute of Child Health and Human Development. (2000). *Teaching children to read: An evidence-based assessment of the scientific research literature on reading and it implications for reading instruction* (Report of the National Reading Panel, NIH Publication No. 00-4769). Washington, DC: U.S. Government Printing Office.

Parish, P. (1963). *Amelia Bedelia*. New York: Harper & Row Trophy Books.

Pearson, D. P. (1982). *Asking questions about stories*. Columbus, OH: Ginn and Company.

Piaget, J. (1974). *The language and thought of the child* (M. Gabain, Trans.). New York: New American Library.

Raphael, T. E. (1982, November). Question-answering strategies for children. *The reading teacher, 36*(2), 42–49.

Roe, B. D., & Ross, E. P. (2006). *Integrating language arts through literature and thematic units*. Boston: Pearson Education.

Rowe, M. B. (1974). Wait-time and reward as instructional variables, their influence on language, logic, and fate control: Part One—Wait time. *Journal of Research on Science Teaching, 11*(2), 81–74.

Rowe, M. B. (1978, March). Wait, wait, wait . . . *School Science and Mathematics, 78*(3), 207–216.

Rowe, M. B. (1986). Wait time: Slowing down may be a way of speeding up! *Journal of Teacher Education, 37*(1), 43–50.

Sadker, D., & Sadker, M. (2003). Questioning skills. In J. Cooper (Ed.), *Classroom teaching skills* (pp. 101–147, 7th ed.). Boston, MA: Houghton Mifflin Company.

Schön, D. A. (1995). *The reflective practitioner.* New York: Basic Books.

Sheldon, D. S., & Blythe, G. B. (1997). *The whales' song.* London: Puffin Books.

Stabile, C. (2001). *Improving the performance of sixth-grade social studies students through exposure to philosophy* [Doctoral dissertation, Nova Southeaster University]. (ERIC Document Reproduction Service No. ED 469 402)

Steil, K., Summerfield, J., & DeMare, G. (1983). *Listening: It can change your life.* New York: McGraw-Hill.

Stevenson, C. (1986). *Teachers as inquirers: Strategies for learning with and about early adolescents.* Columbus, OH: National Middle School Association.

Strickland, D. S., Galda, L., & Cullinan, B. E. (2004). *Language arts: Learning and thinking.* Belmont, CA: Wadsworth/Thomson Learning.

Taba, H., Levine, S., & Elzey, F. F. (1964). *Thinking in elementary school children.* U.S. Office of Education, Department of Health, Education and Welfare, Cooperative Research Project No. 1574. San Francisco: San Francisco State College.

Thompson, K., Leintz, P., Nevers, B., & Witkowski, S. (2004). *The integrative listening model: An approach to teaching and learning listening.* University Park: Penn State University Press.

Tobin, K. (1987, Spring). The role of wait time in higher cognitive level learning. *Review of Educational Research, 57*(1), 69–95.

Tomlinson, C. (1999). *The differentiated classroom: Responding to the needs of all learners.* Alexandria, VA: Association for Supervision and Curriculum Development.

Tomlinson, C., & McTighe, J. (2006). *Integrating differentiated instruction & understanding by design (Connecting content and kids).* Alexandria, VA: Association for Supervision and Curriculum Development.

Van Allsberg, C. (1986). *The stranger.* Boston: Houghton Mifflin Company.

Vygotsky, L. S. (1962). *Thought and language.* Cambridge: M.I.T. Press.

Waber, B. (1972). *Ira sleeps over.* Boston: Houghton Mifflin.

Walsh, J. A., & Sattes, B. D. (2005). *Quality questioning.* Thousand Oaks, CA: Corwin Press.

Wilen, W. W. (1991). *Questioning skills for teachers: What research says to the teacher* (3rd ed.). Washington, DC: NEA Professional Library. (Eric Document Reproduction Service No ED332983)

Wolfe, P. (2001). *Brain matter: Translating research into classroom practice.* Alexandria, VA: Association for Supervision and Curriculum Development.

Wood, A. W. (1998). *I'm as quick as a cricket.* Swindon, England: Child's Play Intl Ltd.

Index

About the Author

Esther Fusco is currently an associate professor at Hofstra University in Hempstead, New York. She is the chair of the Department of Teaching, Literacy, and Leadership. She served as an adjunct at Hofstra for 15 years before becoming a full-time faculty member. Before coming to Hofstra, Dr. Fusco was the principal of the Port Jefferson Elementary School for 8 years and the principal of the Babylon Elementary School for 8 years. In Babylon, she also served as the director of Curriculum K–12 and the director of Special Education. In addition, Dr. Fusco was a Middle School Reading Coordinator and Elementary Gifted Coordinator in the Shoreham Wading River School District. Currently, Dr. Fusco is the facilitator for the ASCD (Association for Supervision and Curriculum Development) National Network on Language, Literacy, and Literature and the chair of the Balanced Literacy Special Interest Group for the International Reading Association. Dr. Fusco has authored several children's literature programs, numerous articles on curriculum and instruction, and a series of books on portfolio assessment.

In 2006, Dr. Fusco was named New York State Elementary School Principal of the Year by the State Association of Administrators of New York, and she was awarded the title of National Principal of the Year by the National Association of Elementary School Administrators and the U.S. Department of Education. Additionally, she received the Hofstra University Teacher of the Year Award.